The ETIQUETTE of Kindness

IT'S NOT JUST ABOUT THE RIGHT FORK!

Skills and Courtesies for Our Time

A Manual for Young People (and Others!)

SUZANNE-MARIE ENGLISH

Illustrations by Alexander Orion Sparks

The
Etiquette of Kindness
It's Not Just About the Right Fork!
Skills and Courtesies for Our Time
A Manual for Young People (and Others!)

By Suzanne-Marie English
Artwork, Alexander Orion Sparks
Copyright © 2012 by Suzanne-Marie English
All rights reserved.

Published by Pleasant Ranch Publishing
P.O. Box 10
Rescue, CA 95672
ISBN 1479181404
ISBN 9781479181407

First printing: November, 2012
Printed in the United States of America
First Edition: November, 2012

Available through your favorite bookseller or online from Amazon.com
Further information or bulk purchase inquiries:
www.etiquetteofkindness.com

To all young people seeking
Life skills and opportunities.

Contents

Etiquette!

It May Have Seemed Like It Was About the Right Fork... But It Was Mainly About Kindness All Along!

The Etiquette Adventure!

What a journey! Who would have guessed that there could be such passion hidden in *etiquette!*

Over the past fifteen years and more, I've had the fun and satisfying opportunity of sharing door-opening, happiness and confidence-making Etiquette Classes with hundreds of young people. We've laughed and learned together as I've observed many of these mainly sixth, seventh and eighth graders go from hesitant students, not sure about "this etiquette stuff", to eager kids with increased confidence in their social skills and in their roles as compassionate, caring human beings.

This has been fabulous for me! I've seen my passion for the door-opening possibilities of kindness-based, confidence-building, learned etiquette skills ignite young people of varying personalities.

I've had the honor of seeing *shy* and more hesitant young persons gain the security and happy confidence to handle themselves in situations they were unsure of before our classes together.

I've had the fun of watching the more *outgoing* students blossom as well, perhaps gaining a quieter, more solid assurance that they know how to handle situations; perhaps finding a deeper sense of compassion that they then transmit in their outward actions.

All students gained confidence in knowing what to do to open those *doors of possibility!*

Catching Fire with Kindness!

When I began teaching the Etiquette Classes, it quickly became clear to me that together we were learning and practicing so very much more than *just etiquette!* Everything we learned had to do with *I-Thou*, the *circularity* of good, caring communication and interaction, the respect for likenesses and differences. We realized that our etiquette endeavors had to do with trying to treat each other as we'd like to be treated – with helping each other with *kindness.*

It was that kindness-factor that the kids heard, practiced and loved – I could see them *catch fire with kindness!* I found that deeply moving.

Oh, the Fun of It!

The students loved our role-playing! We'd start off each Etiquette Class with acted-out examples by their teacher and me. They loved seeing us get up there first, making up spontaneous scenes of the *scream-in-the-night-bad* examples of behavior. Amid much laughter, the students would then critique our performances of awful etiquette, making observations of what was wrong, harsh, inappropriate or discourteous. Then it was the students' turn to act roles!

They would eagerly ask to play-act our etiquette topic, taking great delight in broadly playing the *bad examples*. They took pride in showing *how it's done* as we refined and determined what the *kinder*, more skillful approach might be in the subject of our etiquette lesson of the day.

The students' obvious delight with their newly-acquired skills and the confidence they could feel themselves gaining kept us joyfully learning and sharing from week to week.

The Etiquette of Kindness *Expands!*

I came to realize that as much as I loved the interaction – and learned so very much from the terrific students and skilled teachers I met – I just couldn't be enough places teaching classes to the numbers of young people I wanted to reach. I needed to add a tool to extend etiquette classes to more students.

The positive responses from the students and the requests from the parents, teachers and home schooling parents wanting this information readily accessible, prompted me to put *The Etiquette of Kindness* in book form.

Because there's so very much to *real* Etiquette – far more than solely table setting or *howdy-do's*, I came up with our very long title:

The
ETIQUETTE
of Kindness

IT'S NOT JUST ABOUT
THE RIGHT FORK!

Skills and Courtesies for Our Time
A Manual for Young People (and Others!)

So, though Etiquette is certainly *not* just about the right fork – it sure helps to know which one to use! Just as our title implies, in our *Etiquette of Kindness* we learn a lot of *Skills and Courtesies for Our Time!*

We broaden our knowledge and social skills, from a good deal about *The Right Fork* (and knives, spoons, plates...!), to creating smooth and interesting introductions, developing skillful communications (including phone usage, texting, e-mail...). We learn to present ourselves as we desire; we learn the art of saying "Please!" and "Thank you!" with sincerity, creativity and good grammar!

It's the Real Deal!

And all the time, in everything we do, in all of our good cheer and learning together, our focus in classes and in this book is on how we treat each other. This is the basis for our interactions – the real deal – *The Etiquette of Kindness!*

The entire journey of sharing and learning with so many wonderful young people, teachers and parents has been a delight. It's fabulous to be now taking this adventure of meaningful etiquette broader and broader, with opportunities to meet and greet and interact all along the way!

It is my hope that *The Etiquette of Kindness – It's Not Just About the Right Fork!* with its *Skills and Courtesies for Our Time*, can be of service as a helpful, confidence-building and easily accessible *Manual for Young People (and Others!)*.

Who would have guessed? Etiquette, it turns out, is an adventure and just plain *fun!*

<u>Note:</u> In setting up the form of this book, I came to realize that it would also be helpful if young people, their teachers and families could easily use it as a simple reference or workbook. For that reason, I've included, at the ends of most chapters, a section for further consideration, practice, contemplation, research, discussion or role playing opportunities. The table of contents notes the pages on which those sections start for each chapter.

1.

Etiquette Inspirations

Why We are Learning About
The Etiquette of Kindness Together!

Etiquette – it's a strange word, isn't it?

In the short, easy definition, it just means an identified way – or traditionally accepted way – of acting toward other people within our group.

Even more simply: *etiquette* refers to how we treat one another – our *behavior* toward each other.

This fancy-sounding word, *etiquette*, filtered down to us from *Old French* words: *estiquette,* meaning *label* and *estiquier,* meaning *to attach.*

From that origin, we've come to regard *etiquette* as the customs, forms or rules of behavior we've selected (labeled) to use and to *attach* to our group, whether it's our ethnic, community, country, social, business, professional or religious group.

It's Practical – Usually!

Some of the *rules* of etiquette seem to make good sense when we think about them; others may seem really weird or seem like they'd make absolutely no difference if we forgot about them! But many of our etiquette traditions *do* make sense if we are using etiquette's so-called *rules*, forms or guidelines in an instance appropriate for them – and in the particular group for which they were intended!

As a general guideline, the more formal a situation, the more etiquette rules are applied and the more care we take in using the appropriate form of etiquette for the social setting. (I personally know several young people who in their teens and twenties either ended up having tea with The Queen of England or being introduced to The President of the United States! Were they glad they knew social graces and more formal etiquette! Life has a way of sending us surprises, and it's always nice to be ready!)

For our *Etiquette of Kindness* purposes here, we will learn somewhat about the *very* formal ways of etiquette. Generally, however, we will be learning the basics-and-then-some of etiquette skills. These skills will see us through in just about all circumstances we might normally encounter – and they would certainly set us up skillfully and confidently for more formality if needed.

We will concentrate on learning how to present ourselves well, how to treat others in social settings and how to adapt graciously, courteously and *kindly* in nearly any situation in which we find ourselves as we go along in life!

These useful Etiquette Skills we gain will help us to be resourceful – to confidently think on our feet – and to respond graciously to situations as they arise.

Good Etiquette Helps Doors Open!

Etiquette skills are tools, and, just like any other tools we've learned to use, they help us to do things when and how we want them done. Our skillful ability to *do things* opens doors of opportunity and experience – it's simple! Etiquette skills are no exception!

Being able to use our tools of etiquette well and appropriately can help us to feel confident and feel happier with ourselves. Good etiquette can help us to be more comfortable and can bring us positive attention — the kind we want!

It's a Tool We Can Use — or Not!

Just as with any tools or skills, we can always choose to use our etiquette skills — or not.

But, if we are clueless as to how to do something — or if we haven't an idea about how to behave in a given situation — we sure can't pull it out of the air in a pinch!

Not having adequate social skills limits us; having them and practicing them makes us ready for opportunities!

Mindful Kindness!

Practicing these etiquette skills brings us more pleasant daily social interactions, increases our self-confidence and helps to open doors of opportunity for ourselves — and graciously holds the doors of opportunity open for others.

Since everyone wants to feel good, no matter the differences in life experiences, opportunities or traditions, a little or a lot of kindness goes a long way.

Then, when we choose to mindfully use our etiquette skills *in kindness,* it becomes a very big deal, indeed: The *Etiquette of Kindness* put into practice helps to create a good, happy and meaningful life for us and for others!

Treating Others as We Believe We'd like to Be Treated

In our Etiquette of Kindness endeavors we always try to consider and respect that there are various ethnic and family traditions. We realize that:

- *Not every social skill we learn is universally accepted or useful.*

- *Not everyone's experiences in Life are the same as ours.*

However, the desire to be treated with kindness *is* common to us all. So, though we can never walk exactly in another person's path, we try to treat others as we would like to be treated — and we are grateful for kindness and consideration being shown to us.

We do our best in a good, positive spirit — and *trust* that others also act from this sort of attitude.

We know that we — and others in their turn — will be imperfect in attempts at kindness, but still, we offer kindness and courtesy genuinely and most often we find this comes to us as well.

However, it's not the *return* that prompts us to be kind: kindness, consideration, gratitude, courtesy — each is its own reward.

Extending these qualities to others as best we can do and determine not only provides good positive feelings *out there*, but it also automatically makes us happier — more creative, more expansive in our brains and more peaceful in our hearts and minds.

And, there's additional good news: as we live more kindly, we realize that it's more fun to act in kindness!

This all adds up to excellent reasons for learning and practicing The Etiquette of Kindness!

It's pretty simple. *The Etiquette of Kindness* is basically learning a few skills and remembering to treat others as we believe we'd like to be treated.

Let's get going!

2.

Commune-icating!

(Or: It's Not All About ME — It Takes Two — or More!)

So! We have great news about something that's really important to us!

We hurry to a special longtime friend to tell her about it. We check with her to make sure she's not busy. We tell her our big news — and it falls flat.

We get no response.

Well, no response other than "Hmmm…" and "Hmm…Oh, that's nice."

We add a bit more information, rounding out the story of this good thing that is important to us, thinking that maybe we haven't been clear or that we've not made our telling interesting enough. Our friend gives us a smile, nods and repeats "That's nice."

Yikes! What's happening? We can't believe this! We can't imagine treating *her* in this way were she delighted with some news of hers and wanted to share with us!

We feel unheard. Unsatisfied. Foolish for having even mentioned anything. Embarrassed with having shared. Frustrated and a bit put out and maybe even angry – with our self for having shared in the first place, and with our friend for showing us such uncaring disinterest!

Though our feelings are hurt right now, we make a mental note to be certain that we never do the same to another – that we kindly show interest instead when a friend or family member wants to share news that's important to her or him! We consider ways that we might show interest and caring.

It Would Have Been Nice

We would have liked to have had a question or two asked about our good news; maybe some enthusiasm, too, from our friend. A bit of dialogue about this subject that is important to us would have been nice. Just some show of caring interest would have meant so much!

We tried to share – to *communicate* – but it fell miserably flat and un-received!

Our disappointment is understandable since

Communication Is a Big Part of Life – And It's *Actively Circular!*

Communicate comes from *to commune: to share; to interact; to make known; to relate with depth of feeling.*

Consider the important words that spring from *commune* – words that we use every day:

Communicate
Communication
Community
Communion

Just think about it! All of these words indicate:

> Back-and-forth
> Conversation
> Circularity
> An attitude of *us*...

...not "Me! Me! Me!" without hearing or considering *you!*

These words all have to do with sharing ourselves; with interacting with others, with our environment and with the places where we live, work and play. These words are involved with our sense of spirit or beliefs. They speak of *being present*, either in attitude, intention, interest, involvement or dedication, or in actual bodily placement as "I live in a great community."

Communication is alive and vital! It moves, weaves and circulates! Let's make sure that *our* communication efforts are honest, kindly and trustworthy; that they carry sincerity of attitude, positive intent and helpful content!

It's an Honor to Communicate in Respect and Consideration!

We can *commune*-icate — truly connect — with others! We can learn to be skillful and thorough in our communication; to communicate satisfyingly, happily and honorably with generosity, respect and loving kindness.

Any efforts we put toward becoming better communicators are efforts well-placed since communicating is a wondrous, basic part of human life! So — *let's get it down!*

Our Communications Basics!
<u>In person</u>

- We *turn our body toward* the person or people with whom we are speaking.

- We stand with our body *open,* meaning that we don't cross our arms over our chest. This is receptive *body language* in most Western cultures, indicating that we are listening to the other person and to what he or she has to say!

- We *look directly* at the other person or persons with whom we are talking.

- We *smile* (unless it's something very serious being shared, of course!), perhaps incline our head in the direction of the person speaking.

- We *listen actively,* meaning that we listen quietly but might ask a question when appropriate. When there is a space in the conversation, we might give a bit of our own observation or make short comments that show interest and build on the other person's comments.

- We *don't take calls or texts* while we are in conversation with another person! Rare exceptions might be: awaiting a call in an emergency/critical situation; awaiting a call that affects us and our conversation partner, and we both understand the necessity. (Please see our chapter 4, *Saying "Hi!" Electronically! Telephone Etiquette...* for further ideas on this.)

Over-the-phone/video chat

> If we are not communicating in person but over the phone or by video chat, much of what we've mentioned in the list above still works for good communication:

- We keep our body *open* and in a listening/interested posture.

- We *listen actively,* as above, with comments or questions offered when there's an appropriate space to do so — but we don't *interrupt.*

- We show our friend, loved-one or acquaintance *respect* by just doing the *one thing* at the moment — talking with him/*commune-icating!*

- We don't rudely go online to *browse* or play a game or text on another phone while we are talking with the original person. (That *distracted* communication can be heard in our voice and it's hurtful and insulting to the other person!)

- And, when appropriate (which is much of the time), we *have a smile in our voice by having a smile on our face!*

Let's Revisit!

With what we know about good communication, we'll go back to our first example — that unsuccessful, non-communication — and take it again, from a better, kinder perspective. Okay!

We have what we consider to be a neat idea or interesting or important news to share with our friend. We are eager to share it with her, so we call or mention it when we see her. And, oh happy satisfaction! When we share this information, we get a courteous, interested response!

If we communicated *in person,* our friend turned toward us, smiled appropriately and warmly welcomed us by her *body language!* We felt good! It made us glad that we *shared — not embarrassed to have spoken!*

Perhaps she included such phrases as:

"Oh, that's interesting! What happened then?"

"I had no idea! Please, tell me about it!"

"Hmm…Tell me more!"

"What made you think of that?"

"That's terrific! When are you going?"

"Oh, I'm so sorry about that! How did it make you feel? Were you surprised?"

"Wow! How'd that happen?"

"Oh, gee, I'm not so sure I see it that way…What made you think that?"

And then we answered thoughtfully and thoroughly, and our friend responded again with further comments or other questions or observations. *Voilà!* We have *communication!*

There has been a *back-and-forth* between us. We have created a *conversation* — we *have communicated!*

Now, how does this feel?

Probably, in our second example, we feel satisfied, happy that we shared and *safe* with our ideas, opinions or news.

With that satisfying exchange, we and the other person have created possibilities for further communication, enjoyment and growth — always good things!

It's SO Worth the Effort!

Positive interaction — real *commune*-ication activity — is of value in all relationships, including those of friendship, school, family and business. This approach is health building and dynamic for any type of community group as well, whether a spiritual or interest community, or in our actual neighborhood, town or even a wider regional or world community.

The other person doesn't always have to agree if it's a question of ideas or observations shared, but willingly, actively *hearing* each other is the basis for creating satisfying communication and the possibilities of better understanding.

While none of us is perfect, we can take the time and care to *usually* get our communications right. By using courtesy and thoughtfulness, we will establish ourselves as *someone who cares and is interested in others!* Being this sort of person is always excellent, gives us self-confidence and a good feeling of being a "team player" as we go along in Life.

Commune-icating is a wonderful thing! Used well, it is exciting! It can open doors of possibility and opportunity for us and for others. It's basic to our *Etiquette of Kindness* — it can be *just plain fun!*

Role Playing Opportunities:

Ask another person or several other people to create a *worst case*/awful communication situation with you.

- Have one person be the friend trying to bring the other(s) news that they want to share. (It can be anything you make up.)

- Have another person or persons play-act that they are really bored, disinterested or can't be bothered. Perhaps they look at their fingernails, stare down at the floor, sigh, fiddle with their hair or tap a pencil. Maybe they look up at the ceiling, the sky or off in another direction. Perhaps they barely say anything. (You could even pretend to read and respond to a text coming in – yikes!) Whatever seems to create the bad mood!

- This doesn't have to be long; maybe only for a minute or two at most. (Since it's so unhappy and unsatisfying, it probably won't be long!)

- Talk about how this feels, and then all make observations about how it went and what was missing.

- Now, try it as we've talked about, creating a nice back-and-forth and engaged conversation for a few minutes' practice. Show interest!

- Pay attention to *body signals* such as: looking at the other person as she/ he talks; standing or sitting so your body is directed toward the other; keeping a pleasant, interested look on your face; stopping other activities while you listen.

- Talk about how *this* feels!

Change roles if you care to and try it again. Give everyone a chance for practice; take turns playing both the *good* and the *bad* roles.

Keep it light and have fun!

Note: Additional ideas on communicating are found especially in chapter 4, *Saying "Hi!" Electronically!* as well as in chapter 3, *Making Your Acquaintance! Meeting-and-Greeting...* and in chapter 6, *Thank You! Writing Letters and Notes... Saying "Thanks!" and "Hello!"*

3.

Making Your Acquaintance!

Meeting-and-Greeting: A Basic Life Skill — and Fun!

Meeting new people is an adventure! Sharing treasured friends and loved ones by introducing them to each other and creating relaxed, interesting scenarios for meeting-and-greeting is a valuable, learnable talent. With a little awareness and desire, we can become skillful at introductions.

It's a Gift!

Putting someone at ease in a new situation is a great gift to that person and a basic skill to learn and "perfect". We put quotes around *perfect* because it's important to remember from the outset that everyone messes up in introductions at times. Everyone forgets a name from time-to-time! The important thing is to remember our goal of kindness and thoughtfulness — that's always primary, including in our introductions.

Usually It's Simple but Form CAN Be a Big Deal!

Our starting point in our acquaintance with any other person — our first impression — is the introduction! Most of our daily uses of meeting-and-greeting are quite casual; they follow some basic, simple guidelines of friendliness and consideration. But when it comes to requirements for real formality, the *form* of our introductions becomes especially important. It's quite likely that we will have occasions to be involved in professional introductions, introductions for job opportunities or introductions for college interviews. In any of these situations, we will want to know how to conduct ourselves from the outset — from the introduction!

It's Not Impossible At All!

Life can take turns where we find ourselves in ever-widening circles of interaction and ever-more-formal requirements of Etiquette.

At some period in our lives, we could be included in a super-formal receiving line where introductions are made *very properly* to an international dignitary, to the President of the United States or perhaps to a monarch of England, Japan, Sweden or of some other country. It's not out of the realm of reason to think that we could find ourselves in a particularly formal setting of introductions in any country of the world. It happens!

For instance...

Our interest in world affairs could take us into a profession of diplomacy or international law; our passion for medicine could lead us into practice and research on a world scale; our fascination with science and the environment could take us around the world and into outlying spots. Our business interests might require that we move in international circles, meeting-and-greeting as our responsibilities dictate; our talents with a camera might lead us into all sorts of foreign adventures, meeting villagers and dignitaries alike. All of these, as well as many other situations, would require that we bring ourselves up-to-speed with formal protocol and with international cultural requirements in social and business settings. Knowing how to conduct ourselves formally would become an expected part of our life!

And at any age, if our lives or our family members' lives are intertwined with diplomacy, with high-level government or military protocol or if we are involved with very formal educational settings, our daily routines will have quite formal moments, indeed!

Thankfully, We're Quick Studies!

Since we're here learning good, practical Etiquette together, basic concepts of courteous conduct are not foreign to us.

We are confident that we can meet any etiquette need and quickly catch on to whatever is required, getting up-to-speed in no time at all!

Body Language Is Super Important!

Before we go into further detail — before we talk of formal or casual introductions and before we consider possible cultural exceptions to our traditions — we need to discuss the important role of our *body language* in introductions and in meeting-and-greeting!

Whether we are making the introductions, or are part of a group being introduced:

- We smile!

- We stand with our body turned toward the other person or persons, showing interest.

- We keep our body open with no arms crossed over our chest or hands locked behind our back.

- We speak clearly.

- We make certain that we give and receive everyone's names correctly and ask for a name to be repeated if necessary!

- We make direct eye contact. (We address cultural exceptions near the end of this chapter under: *Just When We Thought We Were Getting this Down...*)

- We don't look at the floor or ground or up at the ceiling or sky – nor off over someone's shoulder, checking for who's coming along of more interest to us!

- We give our *active attention* – we certainly don't take or make a call or text during this time!

- We *do* offer our hand in a greeting handshake if that seems comfortable, welcoming and appropriate to the situation – which is most of the time in Western culture. (Find more on this under the heading: *Our Western Handshake,* further along in this chapter.)

Let's continue, now. And for some fun, let's...

Take It from the Top!

To get the idea of what could/might happen in a life situation, we'll start with a fairly formal introduction scenario.

Let's say we have occasion to be asked to introduce another person to our congressperson or to our governor – or even (it could happen!) to the President of the United States who is making a tour of our town, looking at disaster-preparedness programs. We would know what to do! We would make introductions something like this:

"Mr. (or Madam) President, *may I introduce* Mrs. Helen Rodriguez? Mrs. Rodriguez is Chairwoman of our local Red Cross." *The President would extend* his/her hand and the two would shake hands while the President would greet the person being introduced, perhaps saying something like: "Mrs. Rodriguez, I'm happy to meet you; you're doing a fine job here! I've really enjoyed seeing your group's outstanding emergency relief planning!" To which Mrs. Rodriguez would respond, for instance: "Thank you, Mr. (or Madam) President (or President [last name]); I'm so happy to meet you! We are honored that you could join us today. Thank you for coming!"

Two points of special interest in the above setting are:

1. It's always preferred that we ask the person-of-honor's permission to introduce another to him/her; therefore, we use the words *may I introduce* to make our introductions.

2. *The President* in our little snapshot story *extended his (her) hand to offer a handshake*. The point to make is that in cases of formality, or in more traditional ideas of Western handshaking, the elder person (or the person of honor) will decide if a handshake is in order and extend her/his hand to initiate it.

But Casually-Speaking

For most of us, our daily routines don't require that we are involved in extremely formal introductions and formal etiquette requirements.

But most people in any casual setting will still want to feel comfortable and skilled with making introductions, so we'll share some examples here. Our examples will include some possible basic scenarios for introductions, along with suggestions on how we can, at the same time, help create interesting conversational opportunities as well.

First Things First!

We'll want to get pretty secure with these four basic name use scenarios in introducing people:

1. <u>A young person is being introduced to an adult</u>
   The adult's last name will always be included, and the young person will address the adult as introduced, i.e. Mrs./Ms/Mr./Dr... It will be the *adult's option* to have the young person call him/her by a first name.

2. <u>A young person is introducing adults to other adults</u>
   The young person will always use the last names of all the adults being introduced. If any of the adults then wants the other adults or the young person to call him/her by a first name instead, that

adult will make it clear; otherwise, again, we don't presume to use the first name/names.

3. <u>A young person is introducing young persons to other young people</u>
    Last names may or may not be included, but we consider using them when we know them, and especially when we are introducing someone totally new to our friend or into a group of our friends.

4. <u>Adults introducing other adults</u>
    When adults are introducing other adults, they will use first and last names.

A Special Note Here, Please!

Please note that in many examples to come, we don't just give the nuts-and-bolts basics of name only! We try to include small bits of information when we are making our introductions. This helps to create a framework describing how we know the various people and provides possibilities for conversation. This small amount of extra effort takes a sterile "This is…" *so-called-introduction* into something interesting and memorable that shows we care about what we are doing and about the people involved!

Okay! On with our introductions — and do note the extra info that many of our portrayals of good introductions include.

More Introductions Basics!

We'll add a few more basics to keep in mind as we go along:

• We try to say "May I introduce…" rather than "…here's my…" or "…this is…"

• *Pointing out* the person we want to introduce, as in *here is* or *this is,* tends to *objectify* — it treats the person we are introducing as an *object* to be spoken about, not as a human person in our presence to be *honored* with introducing!

• *Ladies are asked permission* to have a gentleman introduced *to them.*

Men are almost always introduced TO women (Note: There are exceptions for *super*-rank if the person holding the apparent position of higher "rank", as in business or politics, is a man. For instance, "Congressman Gonzales, may I introduce my mother, Kathy Robins, the director of our Center for Women and Children?")

In general, men and our friends or younger persons are always intro-duced TO ladies, for instance –

"Mother, *may I introduce* Lily's dad, Dr. Greg Sanders? Dr. Sanders, this is my mother, Kathy Robins."

Mother would most likely extend her hand and say, "Dr. Sanders, I'm so happy to meet you! Lily is a delightful girl and such a good friend of my daughter, Alice!"

Dr. Sanders would say something similar to this as he shakes *mother's* offered hand, "Mrs. Robins, it's my pleasure! Please call me Greg. Our family has been very happy to get to know Alice; she speaks so highly of you and the rest of her family..."

- Young men or boys are always introduced TO young women or girls.

"Jackie, may I introduce Fred and Raymond? We're in English together."

"Ellen and Lucinda, I'd like to introduce my little brother and sister, Nate and Stella; Nate, Stella – Ellen and Lucinda are on swim team with me."

Or, perhaps "Ellen and Lucinda, I'd like my little brother, Jack, and my little sister, Stella, to meet you."

(Notice that preferably we don't say: "Ellen and Lucinda, *this is* my little brother and sister, Jack and Stella." Pointing them out rather than actually introducing them, makes *Jack* and *Stella* seem like some sort of *exhibits – objects –* instead of real people who count!)

- When we want to introduce younger people to adults, we generally ask the permission of the older person to introduce the younger to them.

  "Grandma, may I introduce my good friends, Kate and Sam? I've known them since elementary school! Kate, Sam, my grandmother, Mrs. Kramer."

- As we touched on earlier above, in social or business introductions, so-called *rank* or placement counts. We ask the highest-ranking person who *owns* the setting or situation (no matter the gender or age) if we *may introduce* another person to her/him.

  In our school classroom then, our teacher is *top-person* under normal circumstances, and we introduce everyone to her or him.

  "Mr. Benson, may I (or "...I'd like to...") introduce my grandparents, Mr. and Mrs. Gilroy; they are just moving here from Seattle, and my family and I are so happy they could make it in time to come to our Grandparents' Day!"

  Smiling, *Mr. Benson* would *first* offer his hand to *Mrs. Gilroy*, then to *Mr. Gilroy* to exchange handshakes while warmly greeting them, saying such as:

  "Mrs. Gilroy, Mr. Gilroy, I'm so happy to meet you! How wonderful for you to be able to join us! Thank you for coming. I know Sally is thrilled that you could be here for Grandparents' Day... Have you had a chance to see Sally's work?"

  But, if we were in our grandparents' home, we'd introduce our teacher *to them*, since not only are they the elders, but they are welcoming guests in their own home. We might use wording close to this:

  "Grandma, Grandpa, you remember my teacher, Mr. Benson? Mr. Benson, you met my grandparents, Mr. and Mrs. Gilroy, at our Grandparents' Day."

The three adults would shake hands while *grandma* and *grandpa* greet *Mr. Benson*. They would go on from there, joining in building a pleasing conversation, asking questions and showing interest in each other.

Notice in our example above, *Sally* makes certain that everyone is reminded of each others' names; she doesn't take for granted that each person will remember the others' names, just because they met on a previous occasion.

Mother is *Queen,* Dad is *King!*

In her home and out-and-about with our young friends, our mother is *queen* and we introduce our friends and guests *to her!* Likewise, our dad is *king* and we introduce our friends *to him!*

In our first parent-introductions example here, we are out shopping and meet a couple of our friends in the store. Please note we put *Mom* first:

> "Mom and Dad, I'd like to introduce my friends, Ray and Mark! I met both of these guys this year in my homeroom class and we have P.E., Spanish and American History together...Mark, Ray, my parents, Mr. and Mrs. Cooper."

> To which *Mark* and *Ray* would each shake hands *first* with Mrs. Cooper then with Mr. Cooper, saying, "Mrs. Cooper, Mr. Cooper, I'm very happy to meet you! We're sure glad that your family moved here this year. Tim's a great addition to our basketball team, too!"

> *Mr. and Mrs. Cooper* might respond with, "Ray, Mark, we've heard good things about you both, ever since Tim got into school here – glad to meet you!"

Or, perhaps, in a different setting:

> "Dad! I'd like to introduce Jimmy and his dad, Mr. Anderson; I know Jimmy and Mr. Anderson from soccer. This is my dad, Fred Brandt."

> *Dad* extends his hand *first* to *Mr. Anderson*, then to *Jimmy*, saying, "I'm very happy to meet you, Mr. Anderson, Jimmy! John really enjoys being on the team with you, Jimmy!"

To which *Jimmy* will say something like, "I'm happy to meet you, Mr. Brandt" and his dad might say, "Hello, Fred; glad to meet you! Please call me James. John is a talented goalie and a good sport; we've enjoyed getting to know him!"

It Can Get a Bit Complicated – Not Impossible, Just a Little Tricky!

Here are some important things to be aware of when it comes to introducing women and getting their names said as they prefer and as they use for themselves:

- Women often will take the last name (surname) of their spouse when they are married – *but not always.*

- Sometimes women keep the last name they were born with (their *maiden name*) and still use that if they marry.

- Some women will always go by their name they use professionally – and never change it; they use it for all purposes social and professional, no matter how their life circumstances may change.

- Sometimes women who have been married and who have occasion to re-marry, will change their last name to reflect their new marriage.

- If a woman has children and has been re-married, it's very possible for the children – or some of the children – to have a different last name from their mother.

Whew! This could be a bit confusing sometimes, but it's not impossible to handle at all!

We can deal with a complex name situation if we are aware that there may be confusion and stumbling as to who is called by what last name:

- We include the last name of a woman we are introducing.

- We say the entire name clearly.

As long as we all put our *Etiquette of Kindness* to work and help each other with names, it's not so very complicated – and there's little opportunity for embarrassment with not knowing who is who!

Here are a couple of examples of being helpful in introductions involving name situations that may seem difficult to navigate – but not so, if we help out while making introductions.

In our first example, we are in the home of *Mrs. Fitzgerald* and we make the following introduction:

"Mrs. Fitzgerald, I'd like to introduce Dr. Marcia Holt. Dr. Holt is married to my uncle, Max Sandoval. She is head of the economics department at Sarah Lawrence College and is visiting us while on sabbatical."

Here's another example:

Anne Jeffers lives with her mom and step dad and she brings her friend, *Sally*, home for dinner. *Anne* introduces *Sally* to her mother who goes by her remarried last name, so *Anne* is sure to clearly state to her friend her mother's name when she introduces her – she doesn't let *Sally* presume or guess the last name *Anne's* mother uses!

> "Mom, I'd like to introduce Sally Gilroy! She's in my class; she and I are working on that big American Revolution project together! Sally, this is my mother, *Mrs. Rooney*"

> *Mom* would extend her hand while saying something like, "Welcome, Sally! I'm so happy you could join us for dinner! Anne's told me how she likes doing this project with you!"

> And *Sally* would smile as she shakes hands with *Mrs. Rooney*. She would be certain to *repeat Mrs. Rooney's* name as in, "Thank you, Mrs. Rooney, for inviting me to dinner! I'm so glad Anne and I could team up on that project – it's huge! Together though, we just may get it done on time!"

Introducing Our Friends to Other Friends

Broadening our circle of friends and acquaintances is a fun and enriching part of our lives – and sharing by introducing our friends, brothers, sisters, cousins, etc. to other friends is one way we do that frequently.

This becomes simple when we remember five things:

1. We smile and look directly at the other person/people.

2. We say everyone's name clearly.

3. We tell something about our friends – old and new – to help everyone have a basis for conversation.

4. If appropriate and it seems comfortable, we extend our hand for a handshake.

5. We ask permission of a young woman to introduce a young man *to her*, using "May I introduce…" or "I'd like to introduce…"

A few examples:

"Lily, I'd like to introduce two of my good friends, Craig and Tom. This is Lily's first day here!" to which Lily might respond: "Hi, Craig! Hi, Tom! I'm glad to meet you! Being new and not knowing anyone is pretty weird!" That's *Craig's* and *Tom's* cue to welcome *Lily* and to say something about not worrying – they'll help her meet other friends, too, and maybe ask her about her old school, etc.

And, if a group of boys and girls is being introduced to *Lily,* it might go something like this:

"Lily, I'd like to introduce some good friends: Patti, Craig, Stephanie and Tom. *Lily Ambrose* has just moved here with her mom, dad and sisters and lives next door to my family now; this is her first day at our school!"

"Hi, Lily!" is said all around, while smiling and making eye-contact. Perhaps *Patti, Craig, Stephanie* and *Tom* offer their hands in greeting, saying, "Hi, Lily,

I'm Stephanie Krauss. I think you're in my English class — welcome!" Or, perhaps, "Hi, Lily, I'm Craig Nokura — we met Saturday at the market, remember? Glad you are here!" On around the friend-circle the introductions would go, until *Lily* has met everyone cordially!

We Greet, Repeat — and Don't Shorten or Change!

As this meeting-and-greeting continues around the circle of old-and-new friends, Lily greets each person, repeating their names (as they were given to her) to help her remember them!

She doesn't shorten, lengthen or change anyone's name to something else. She doesn't decide that *Tom* is *Tommy* — unless he tells her to call him that. She doesn't call *Stephanie* by a shortened name of *Steph* — unless she is told differently!

The *Name's* the Thing!

A person's name — how one is identified — is a basic human uniqueness, as only we *name* and *speak* names! Getting a person's name correct — and having the respect to use it as she or he desires — is basic to human interaction!

We don't change a person's name to something else that we might think is *easier, cuter* or *catchier.*

Modifying people's names from what they call themselves can appear lazy or disrespectful; it can be inappropriate to the circumstances of the social setting or too *familiar* a usage for the circumstances.

So here's the nitty-gritty on how we handle people's names:

- We *pay attention* to how other people call themselves.

- We *use* their names *as they give them to us!*

Let Embarrassment Pass Right on by — Just Take Care of Any Awkwardness!

If we forget a name we've just been given or didn't hear it clearly, we ask for it to be repeated right then and there! People are flattered that we want to get their names correct!

Since all of us need clarification at times and are happy for others to get our names straight, we simply:

- Ask to have a name repeated.

- Listen carefully as the name is re-given.

- *Use the name* in the conversation right at that time to get it *imprinted* in our brain!

No Matter What, We Meet No *Dudes!*

We may like to *occasionally* use some casual slang terms (respectful, please!) when chatting with our friends. However, using *dude* or other slang replacements for a name *doesn't work at all* in introductions!

For all of us who really care about other people and want to ensure that we will remember their names, here are some important things to consider:

- We call the person/people to whom we're being introduced by the names we are given.

- We don't address a new-to-us person as *Dude* as in "Hey, Dude – glad to meetcha!"

- Not repeating the other person's name – but instead substituting it with a catch-all slang substitute, such as *Dude, Man* or *Girl* – will almost guarantee that we don't remember the actual name!

- It's just not flattering to other persons, young or old, when we don't care enough to call them by their real name – even upon our first meeting. That's *really* lazy and rude!

- AND! If we are making introductions among our friends, it will do no one any good if we leave people's names out and substitute with *Dude!*

  "Hey, Dude! I want you to meet Bobby. Dude, this is Roger" makes it a lot harder for each of our friends to remember who the other one is. If we take this approach, two opportunities for hearing names will have been wiped out!

It's far better to say, "Hey, Roger! I'd like you to meet Bobby. Bobby, please meet my friend, Roger."

Even better, because there's interesting and helpful info included, is:

> "Roger! I'd like you to meet my new neighbor, Bobby. Bobby's interested in trying out for our basketball team at school; he's played a lot. Roger's on the team, too – a forward!"

In this last instance, we've given both guys not only each other's names, but also a bit of information for conversation. Giving *no* information nearly always results in embarrassing, awkward silence!

If We Have a Dreaded *Name Brain-Lapse?*

Everyone forgets a name from time to time, and sometimes it might even be that we forget the name of our good friend! Yikes! But, it happens and the very best thing to do is to just fess-up and say something like:

> "Oh, my gosh! I'm having a complete *brain lapse* – how can I be forgetting my best friend's name? *Please help!*"

Just as we would do for her, our friend will understand, kindly and good-humoredly laugh it off and quickly remind us of the forgotten name, going on to join in the introductions and in helping to smooth the way forward in conversation.

Everyone *Loves* to Be Recognized and Called by Name! Handy Ways to Help Us Remember

Besides making certain that we hear names correctly, ask for clarification if we are not sure, and repeat and use the other person's name in our conversation, there are some nice little handy helps for being pretty awesome with name-recall! We'll go over a few right here.

Let's say we are looking forward to being with a group of people we haven't seen in a long time. Whether the group is large or small and in our home or in another environment, we can do a few things to help us put names to the people we've known and enjoyed in the past:

1. If we have a name directory, say from a school or from a church, social or business group, we can get that out and run down the listings, recalling faces that go with the names. (If we have such directories, it's a great idea to save these from year to year.)

2. Or, with no directory at hand, we could spend some moments quietly considering old friends and acquaintances we'll likely see at the event, recalling their names as best we can.

3. When we get into the gathering, we will, of course, say *our* name right off when we smilingly greet old acquaintances whom we know, but don't know well. This gives the other person the chance to also give us her name – and we are off to a very good start to a fun time!

4. If we remember something specifically of interest or of importance to that other person, we will ask about it or comment on it. Remembering – and mentioning – something about the other person is a great, flattering way to begin an *I'm-interested-in-you*-conversation!

    "I'm remembering that you were taking a family trip to BC last summer – was it terrific? I love that area! Did you have some favorite spots?" adds a great opening to conversation with an old acquaintance.

Name-Recall-Geniuses!

If we are in the position sometime in our lives to meet and greet a lot of different people, maybe thousands over the course of a year, with the need to recall hundreds of names and faces (along with info for conversation!), we can become masters at name and information recall.

We will be considered *name-recall-geniuses!*

Here's our sure-fired way:

1. We can make our own little "cheat sheet" directory so when we next see the person/people, we will seem like name and info-remembering geniuses, picking up on our conversation where we last left off!

2. We make brief, helpful descriptive notes in our custom directory that we can quickly scan when the occasion arises. (We can use a physical book or e-book of some sort to make our entries – however we are most comfortable.)

3. When we first meet people who we are pretty certain will be in our lives (professional or social) at some future time again, we can

    a. List their name(s).
    b. Briefly note their physical appearances for our own use to identify them again.
    c. Add their country/town/city where they live.
    d. Also enter a short note about what is really important to those people at the moment, such as developing a new project (company, product, concept); traveling somewhere; having something big happening in their or their loved-ones' lives (like a new baby, going to college, retiring, new marriage, new job/business/home).

4. When we know we'll be with the persons again, before we see them, we can take a look at our handy directory listing we've made, refreshing our memory about the people we'll be re-meeting and about what is important to them.

5. If we are caught off-guard and see someone approaching us whom we know – but whose name we aren't recalling, we can greet him warmly *while stating our name*, ask about how he has been since we last saw him, say sincerely how good it is to see him and (if this fits the situation), tell him how we'll enjoy chatting some more over the next minutes/hours/days...

6. If we are fortunate, when we give our name, he will give us his in return; but if that doesn't happen and we can't exactly recall the name and other info at the time, we don't need to panic, because we'll either admit to a temporary memory lapse and politely ask his name, or...

7. ...All we will need are a few minutes of memory refreshing time with our handcrafted entries! We'll be able to recognize exactly this person we want to recall the very next time we see him; we'll be able to ask him further about things important to him – because we've made notes. We can elaborate on what we know is of interest and catch up on where we left off the last visit. We'll be recognized as the memory geniuses that we truly are!

Our Western Handshake!

Most adults these days like to see a confident, friendly young person who looks the other person in the eye, smiles, speaks up – and isn't shy about extending her or his hand in a handshake. However, there are exceptions and we may be surprised by this from time to time!

• In cases of true etiquette formality and in more old fashioned, stricter or traditional ideas of Western handshaking forms, it would be considered *rude,* or *too forward,* for a young person to extend his or her hand before being offered a handshake by the *elder* or *person of authority* being introduced.

• In very formal situations, such as in our meeting and introducing of The President of the United States scenario earlier in our chapter, we would wait upon the person of rank to offer his or her hand in a greeting; we would then continue with our friendly, firm handshake and direct eye contact.

Thankfully for most of our daily involvements, being our confident, friendly, handshake-offering self works just fine! So we'll continue on that basis in our day-to-day life until events take us to other cultures or into a very formal occasion. And then, because we are kind, caring, courteous and smart, we'll be prepared! We'll be informed and ready to adapt and simply do what is needed at the time, showing we are courteous and caring. Easy!

Just When We Thought We Were Getting This Down: *Not* All People in Every Culture or Country Shake Hands *or* Make Direct Eye Contact!

As we've said, in some cultures and social circles, it's considered rude and too forward for young people to offer their hand before an adult would extend his or hers.

And, in some cultures and countries around the world, handshaking isn't done at all! It's customary in some places for men to heartily embrace each other, perhaps with a kiss of greeting to each cheek. However, women and men would *not* greet each other with any physical contact at all. Women meeting women in these cultures might embrace and kiss cheeks or shake hands.

In some countries and cultural traditions, making direct eye contact upon meeting is considered too bold, invasive and rude; the eyes are averted and a formal greeting is given with possibly a handshake – or the greeting is made without a handshake or any physical contact.

In the formal traditions of some cultures, while saying a greeting, a slight polite bow is given with just subtle eye contact and a pleasant smile. This greeting includes no handshake, or physical exchange.

In some cultures and countries, extending an arm around the other person's shoulders, or putting a hand on an arm, is considered far too forward for any greeting situation.

And, at the other end of what's considered *good* and *acceptable* and *expected,* it's not at all unusual in some cultures (and is considered the correct friendly thing) for the men *and* women to heartily embrace each other in greeting. All exchange hugs, the men clap each other on the back, with *hellos* and cheek-kisses exchanged all around!

Sometimes Different – Sometimes Confusing Always Interesting!

Life and traditions – what's considered *acceptable* or *friendly* and *courteous* – can certainly differ, can't they? It can be confusing sometimes – but it's always interesting!

If on occasion we are not sure about meeting-and-greeting; if we anticipate interacting in a social or cultural sphere new to us; if we are traveling into another part of the world and meeting very different cultures, then:

- We need to inform ourselves of the cultures in which we will be circulating and interact according to what their etiquette requires!

- We can do some easy research online or at the library, getting the social etiquette outlines for the country or culture we need.

- Unless it's a situation that comes up *out-of-the-blue,* we will try to be as prepared as possible, so we can relax – and help others to be at ease.

Always, no matter where we are, we keep a certain *attitude of friendliness and respect* in all we do and toward everyone we meet – it's basic to our *Etiquette of Kindness!* This attitude can be felt, seen and heard by others, no matter their apparent differences from ourselves. Our willing, respectful friendliness can help make up for any small lacks in precise social form.

We Can All Help Each Other!
The Etiquette of Kindness Is Circular!

If it's pretty apparent that a friend or acquaintance is having momentary trouble remembering our name so she can make introductions, we can help by offering our name in a smiling, friendly manner which also opens a conversation:

"Hi, Ronald!" (Or just "Hi!" or "Hello!" if we don't know the name yet.) "I'm Helen and I'm so happy to meet you! I've heard such good things about the work you are doing in wildlife rescue!"

Our human interactions are opportunities to include others and to participate in making everyone feel welcome and comfortable. Our meeting-and-greeting skills are prime examples of our *Etiquette of Kindness* at work!

Let's Recap!

We'll gather the basics of our general Western culture introductions here one last time:

- We smile and look directly at the person we are addressing.

- We keep our body *open* — that is, turned to the person(s) we are introducing or to whom we are being introduced.

- We say everyone's name clearly.

- We repeat the other person's name as it's given to us.

- We introduce other people *to* the most senior (in authority or in age) and start by addressing that person, asking "May I...?"

- We extend our hand for a handshake.

- We give a bit of information about the people we are introducing, creating conversation and interest opportunities.

- We respect and observe the cultural differences with meeting-and-greeting.

- We educate ourselves before we are in a situation that requires knowledge of differing cultural traditions and social skills.

- We maintain an attitude of respect and friendliness with all whom we meet.

And Most Importantly!

Since we all like to feel that we *fit in,* helping each other to be more comfortable, and expanding relationships and Life opportunities are basic, very good, happy things indeed! They are an essential part of our *Etiquette of Kindness!*

> We always remember that meeting, greeting and introducing another human being is *an honor to do and a gift to receive!* It affirms the treasure of being an individual human, of being named, noticed, respected and valued.

Enjoy!

Practice and Role Playing Opportunities:

Go back through this chapter on *Making Your Acquaintance...* and take another look especially at any of the headings dealing with specific scenarios of introductions. These might be ones such as *Introducing Your Friends to Other Friends,* or *Mother Is Queen; Dad is King* or any others that help us with what to do and how to do it in likely introduction situations.

Look at our examples — or make up your own — and then role play some possibilities with classmates, with your family or your friends.

Have a good time together! Create some "worst-case scenarios" — these can be a lot of fun — where someone doesn't pay attention, but rather looks off at the ceiling/sky while being introduced or doesn't help out with names or conversation, mumbles and is just sort of a disinterested *lump.*

Laugh a lot! Swap out your roles and then do it again, eventually having everyone take it seriously, settling down and practicing good, friendly versions of introductions.

Have fun as you learn to be comfortable and skillful in your meeting-greeting-introducing!

4.

Saying "Hi!" Electronically!

Telephone Etiquette, Texting, Online Social Networking, E-Mailing — All the Ways We E-Communicate!

Being able to communicate easily and quickly is a handy, useful and helpful thing! Since any form of satisfying, successful communication is about sharing courtesy and consideration, as well as information, we want to remember our *Etiquette of Kindness* skills *even* when we phone, text and e-mail.

No matter what's to come in the evolution of communicating electronically, the basics of thoughtfulness and kindness will always be important factors in any mode of communications with others.

And, being a courteous, accomplished communicator electronically is not a chore or boring; it's fun and it's another important skill that we'll be glad and proud to have!

First Things First: It's NOT Just About Me!

Before we go very far here, it's important to mention that when we make a call or text we are *interrupting* another person. We are asking a person to stop whatever she or he is doing to answer us and our needs, so we always call or text with *respect and courtesy!*

When we contact someone, it's NOT all about just getting what we want!

Because this is a form of communicating with another individual, we use the *Etiquette of Kindness* skills we have learned in face-to-face situations. We remember that communicating, even electronically, is *circular* and about pleasant, considerate human interactions – and not just about satisfying ourselves.

Because It's Circular!

With this *circularity* of communication in mind, it becomes easy to realize that when another person attempts communicating with us, that communication is not complete or satisfying until we do our part!

As thoughtful, courteous individuals interacting with friends, family members and acquaintances it's our responsibility to *acknowledge* and *respond* to someone else's communication.

At our *first opportunity* we will at least acknowledge any e-mails, texts or phone messages. It's rude and *unkind* to just let a person's attempt at interaction *hang out there*, unanswered! If at the moment we don't have time to talk or respond as completely as we'd like or as is called for, we courteously acknowledge the communication and let the caller or sender know that we'll communicate more thoroughly as soon as we are able.

By beginning with this basis of *circularity* for satisfying communications and by taking responsibility to be *responsive* to the other person, we have an excellent start on becoming a truly skilful, pleasant communicator! It's not difficult.

Okay, now, let's proceed!

Suggestions for Telephone Etiquette

Whether we are making or receiving a call, the basics of communicating by any kind of phone are:

1. Identification

2. Courtesy

3. Friendliness

4. Information

1. We always *identify* ourselves, *first thing!*

   Even with the fairly common ability to identify callers electronically, it's still courteous and a basic requirement of telephone manners to identify ourselves by clearly *saying our name when we call someone!* "Hello, Mrs. Ferguson, this is Jason…" or "Hello! This is Jason…" are examples of the most basic beginnings to any phone call we make. First of all, we identify ourselves!

2. We use *courtesy* in making and in receiving phone calls!

   The person who answers the phone is a real person, not just a means to an end!

   In making a personal call, it is courteous and appreciated when we:

- take a few moments to inquire about the well being of the person answering the phone

- ask "May I …?"

- use "please" and "thank you"

- ask if it's a good time to talk

  Our good opportunity may not always coincide with the other person's timing. So, if we are expecting to engage in a fairly lengthy conversation or visit, we ask if it's a good time to talk.

If a call is made at an inconvenient time, we can make plans to talk at a later time.

When receiving a call:

- We are courteous, not showing irritation or impatience at being interrupted!

- We use *courtesy* in asking for the caller's name if he or she neglects to identify him or herself and we don't recognize the voice. We might say, "I'm sorry, I didn't catch your name."

- We *treat the caller with respect and friendliness*, even if she or he is not calling for us!

- When a caller is asking for another person and neglects to give her/his name we can say "Who may I say is calling, please?"

- We are courteous in getting information if we need to take a message and we *write it down!*

- We thank the person for calling and say "goodbye."

3. <u>We communicate *friendliness* when calling – or when receiving a call!</u>

Whether we are making a call *or* receiving it:

- We *smile* when talking to the other person! Our smile can be heard loud and clear! (Radio and television people know this; they use a smile to make their voice convey friendliness and to elicit positive responses in their audience ratings!)

- In a few simple words, we show that we are *interested* in the other person, asking how he/she is and listening to the response.

- "Hello, *Mrs. Ferguson*. This is *Jason*. How are you?"

- "Oh, really? I'm sorry to hear that. I'm glad you're feeling better!"

- OR, perhaps "I heard about your new car (vacation plans, etc.). Do you like it?" "Oh, I'm glad!"

- "I was wondering if *Cindy* is at home and could come to the phone?"

- "Thank you. I'm happy to wait."

- OR, "Oh, she's not home? Well then, would you please tell her I called? Yes, she knows my number. Thank you!"

4. <u>We give and ask for *information* to make the call complete.</u>

   If we are the caller, we clearly give our name, the purpose of our call and, if necessary, a number at which we can be reached.

   If we are taking a call for ourselves or for another person and if the call requires further action, *we write the information down!*

- We get the name, asking "Please, may I have your name again?" or "May I ask who's calling?" and if there's any question, we ask for the spelling.

- We write down the phone number, repeating it to make certain that we have it correctly.

- We take a brief message, stating the purpose of the call; we repeat the information to the caller.

- When we hang up, we note the date and time of the call, so there is no question about when the call was received.

Keeping Our Cell Phones Civil!

Cell phones are useful, handy tools, but they can be major avenues for rudeness and, if used while driving, prime causes of disaster!

- We can be happy, courteous, safe and civil cell phone users.

- We turn off our phones when required or when appropriate to basic courtesy.

- We DON'T text and drive and DO follow all laws and rules (family) regarding cell phone calls while driving.

- We show courtesy to people in our presence in how we handle cell phone calls and texts.

The Big Turn-Off!

We _turn our phone off_ when in a public place where its ringing or its making any noise whatsoever would be a disturbance. It's a basic civility (and often a stated requirement) that we turn off our phones:

- at the movies

- in a house of worship

- in a live theater performance with reserved seating

- in restaurants

- in someone's home where we are a guest for dinner or a party

- at school and at school functions

- at public meetings

- at most sports games and public functions

On _vibrate_ mode, most phones still make considerable, distracting noise. To be sure we and our cell phone are not rude distractions, we turn it off or put it into _silent mode!_

Remember how bright a cell phone screen is when in a darkened movie theater! In a theater of any kind — phone screens are glaringly distracting to others. If we absolutely must make or check on a call, we leave the darkened theater to do so.

Disastrous Combo!

Take one vehicle. Add a driver (and maybe some passengers!). Add roads to navigate, other drivers, weather conditions and maybe a dog, or a deer. Now add a cell phone, calls to be made or answered and texts to be typed. This all adds up to a combination for disaster! Tragedies that can't be undone by wishes or by tears!

There are many statistics of needless accidents and deaths brought on by drivers who are not *with* their driving mentally, or who are involved in the screen of their phone, looking away "just for a moment" to text or to handle a call!

Putting our own life and the lives of others at risk is unsafe and foolish, the height of selfishness, thoughtlessness and carelessness. It is the very essence of UN-kindness!

So, since we are kind, thoughtful, caring and smart people when it comes time to drive, we just *drive*.

- We DON'T text

- We DO follow the rules of the road and the specific laws regarding distractions such as cell phones, texting, etc.

- We DON'T add handling a phone or texting to the big responsibility of driving!

- We DO find a spot where we can safely and legally leave the roadway, park and take care of any cell phone call or texting.

One Time NOT to Worry About Someone's Feelings!

We will want to decide *before* we get into *anyone's* vehicle that being a passenger doesn't mean giving up our safety and peace of mind! When necessary, we will speak up; we won't stand for any driver driving distractedly, being a fool and putting our life and safety at risk! We should have this resolve firmly in our minds, especially before we ever go out with friends or older siblings!

If we are a passenger in a vehicle where the driver is not paying sufficient attention to his or her driving — perhaps texting or making or receiving phone calls — we *don't hesitate to speak up!*

One possibility to ending the texting/calling distraction might be to offer to take any incoming phone calls for the driver or to text a note for her or him. Some drivers will appreciate our polite, firm offer of taking on that small task while the driver just drives!

In any case, we are not hesitant to let the driver know of our discomfort with less-than-attentive driving! We clearly ask a careless driver to immediately stop phoning or texting and to pay attention only to driving! If the driver refuses and continues the thoughtless, dangerous activity, then we will ask the driver to stop at the first safe place to drop us off!

An unsafe driving situation is NOT a time to be worried about the driver's feelings or sensitivities. It's not a time to be concerned about any names or slights she or he may throw in our direction. It's not a time to care about someone's opinion of us! This is serious!

So, in a case where we find ourselves a passenger in the vehicle of an unsafe distracted driver:

- We clearly state our discomfort with the distracted driving.

- We ask for any distracting activity to be stopped while we are a passenger.

- We demand that a driver who refuses to stop the distracting activity immediately find a public place to safely let us out of the vehicle.

- We use our own cell phone to call home or another trusted person to come pick us up.

Now, from our super-serious, life-and-death considerations regarding phoning and texting, we'll go back to instances where we simply try to avoid being rude! A relief — whew!

Rude Juggling Acts!

If we're having a face-to-face visit with some friends and if the conversation isn't meeting our expectations for being entertained, it's highly unlikely that we'd get out a deck of cards or start thumbing through a catalog or book, saying "Hmm…I know…Is that so?…Well!" as we glance in their direction from time to time!

My, oh my! Just how long might we keep these friends we've treated so insultingly? Likely, not long!

Or, suppose we are having a conversation with one person and another acquaintance of ours shows up. It's very likely we wouldn't abruptly stop our first conversation, turn our back to the first person and start talking exclusively with the new person! But, that's exactly what we do when we take cell phone calls or answer text messages coming in while already engaged in conversation with others!

When we allow our communication devices to interrupt or hi-jack our normally-courteous interactions, it's the same as suddenly turning our back on a person with whom we are visiting! We just wouldn't do that!

Sometimes it's truly amazing how far we've allowed ourselves to go down the path of electronic rudeness when using our e-communication devices.

Talking with one or more persons while texting with someone else, Web surfing or playing an e-game while chatting on the phone and taking a cell phone call while having a face-to-face conversation are all easy contenders for first prize in electronic rudeness.

Yikes! How can we even begin to think that this rude *split* attention is acceptable?

All of these discourteous actions say:

"You certainly are not important or interesting enough for me to give you and your thoughts, your words, your news or your *whatever* my full attention. I do not value you or your time!"

So, since that's certainly NOT what we are about and NOT what we want to convey...

...We Just Don't DO These Things!

Answering cell phones or making calls, texting, playing e-games or surfing the Web are *never* appropriate:

- at the dining table

- in a house of worship

- at public meetings

- in school

- in theaters

- when we are out with family and friends or in any place where our actions regarding electronic communications would be rude, insulting or a distraction

Plain! Simple! Easy!

Okay, now, more specifics — just to be sure we get this!

Talking with One Person — While Texting with Another!

Here are some guidelines for us all when it comes to texting.

1. We don't text while visiting with others!

    We don't fall for thinking that we can be in an actual, *live* conversation with people who are physically present with us in any setting and text to someone else at the same time — it doesn't work! It does show the people with whom we actually are at the time, how very little we value their thoughts, feelings, time or efforts in being there with us!

2. Ideally, we turn off our phones when we are visiting with others in person.

   If for some reason we haven't done that and we hear a text come in, we can do one of a couple of things.

   > We can ignore the incoming message (and get back to it later when we are alone).

   > We can wait for a lull in the conversation – one has probably been made by the sound of our text coming in – and say "I'm sorry. Would you excuse me for a moment, please?" We then either leave the room for a moment or, depending upon the situation and with the "okay" of the other person(s) present, we might make a quick text jot and then immediately return to our conversation.

A Few (Rare) Exceptions

There are some relatively rare situations when we might consider keeping our cell phones at the ready for receiving or sending texts or phone calls, while visiting with others.

If we are waiting for a *truly* important message, we *might* make an exception as long as we are NOT at a formal dinner table, in a movie or other theater or in a house of worship, etc. An exceptional situation would be our parents requiring us to be available for their call, if we are expecting news of an urgent or emergency nature or if we are awaiting a critical message regarding business or employment. (This last situation is usually for adults, but some young people also are in positions of business of some sort.)

In such a case, we would courteously alert the people with whom we are visiting that we may need to deal with an anticipated important text or call. We would use our best sense of courtesy and consideration to excuse ourselves and take care of whatever we need to handle.

Oops! Happen

Sometimes, we are out and about, run into an acquaintance and are just casually talking with her or him when our phone rings or a text message comes in. It happens. Depending upon the situation, we could ignore the call or message and return it later, or we could say, "Excuse me for a sec, please," take the call and then kindly but briefly ask if we can get back to the caller very soon.

> "Hello, Mary! It's so good to hear from you and I'm wondering if I could call you back in a bit?"

This sort of courteous handling of an unexpected call is also appropriate when we are involved with a sales person in a store. If a phone call or text comes in, we treat the person assisting us with the same respect and courtesy and don't turn aside, making her or him wait until we are done talking or texting!

Web Surfing or Game Playing
While Talking on the Phone
Or While Visiting with Someone in Person!

When we are talking with someone, either on the phone or face-to-face, it's basic courtesy to fully engage with that person!

If we are chatting with someone on the phone or in person, it's just plain rude to be also surfing the web or playing a game! This sort of split activity says "You just aren't interesting enough for me to give you my undivided attention!"

So, in person or over the phone, while we are talking with a person, we give her or him our undivided attention. When we are done with our conversation, we can go on to do other things.

Listen to What We Say!

When creating a voice mail greeting for our home or cell phone, we will want to consider that not everyone will appreciate the humor we might share with our friends or buddies!

A caller might be an elder relative, our teacher, a prospective employer or someone we just might not want to treat casually.

We will want to consider that what we think is hilarious, or our trying to add music that we love, may not work as the clever message we intend, but instead may turn out sounding garbled and unintelligible over the phone! That can end up confusing and embarrassing for everyone!

Most of the time, simple, friendly and clear works the best for phone messages; we can still personalize our answering message and have fun with it, if that's our style.

E-Mailing Etiquette

In its own way, using e-mailing to communicate can be really handy and helpful. However we are using this tool, we will want to follow our Etiquette of Kindness guidelines of courtesy and thoughtfulness, using appropriate language, friendly greetings and satisfying closings.

E-mailing is also a good place to practice our better spelling and grammar usage instead of turning to the abbreviations like LOL, OMG, etc., which we might habitually choose in texting!

Using e-mail is great for sending and receiving files (documents or pictures) as attachments! And, when we do that, it's common courtesy to make certain that anything we send as an attachment is virus-free. We can use any of a number of virus-scanning security programs to make our attachments problem-free!

Most of us are not happy with others casually sharing our personal info far and wide. Unless we are e-mailing to a specific friend or family group which naturally interacts as a group via e-mail, we'll want to keep others' e-mail addresses private. So, when we are sending a general e-mail message to multiple, not necessarily connected, recipients it is a common courtesy to *blind copy* to them. In this way, only our e-mail address and name are available for all recipients to view. Taking this extra step of courtesy also helps to keep our communications from becoming unwitting vehicles for dreaded spam!

The Transparency of Social Networks, Texts and E-Mail!

How we conduct ourselves and what we write to express ourselves on social networks, in texts and in e-mails does count!

The apparent casualness and immediacy of e-communication does not make poor behavior somehow *cool!* E-communicating isn't an exception to using kindness, courtesy and thoughtfulness in what we say.

Since all of our words mirror who we are and how we think about ourselves, other people and our world, we want to stick to what we know about our Etiquette of Kindness, *even* when we are e-communicating!

These electronic forms of communication are very personal, very immediate; they mirror our thoughts and feelings at any given moment! When we forget how transparent e-communicating is, our words can become a snare of embarrassment and dismay for ourselves and possibly for others! Oh, my!

And, pressing the *delete* button does not necessarily mean *gone!*

Though our second thoughts may have prompted us to *delete* a comment or to wish we hadn't sent a text, due to the wonders of our electronic communications age, statements we might wish away are not entirely gone! E-comments – those we are proud of and those we'd like to take back – all hang around on archives of social networking sites, blogs and on peoples' computers, phones and devices. Yikes!

E-Etiquette Counts!

Being a skillful, kindly and wise communicator electronically holds the same personal benefits for us as communicating well in any situation; it's a big component to doing well socially and in business.

Good communication skills say about us: This is likely a person who cares, is thorough, courteous and capable.

In every form of communication etiquette counts – and using courtesy and kindness in all of our e-communications is no exception. Our etiquette skills work well for us and for those with whom we talk, text and e-mail. It's just that simple!

No matter how technologically astounding and electronically *whiz-bang* we become in our e-communications, the Etiquette of Kindness will always be the way to conduct ourselves, anytime, anywhere!

Practice and Role-Playing Opportunities!

Practicing our phone manners can be a lot of fun! We can take many of our sections in this chapter and role play with one or several people. We can take turns doing things just terribly — and then switch our role playing around so that we practice how to act, how to call, how to behave in courteous, kindly ways when we e-communicate.

Here are a few possibilities:

- The Frustrating, *Non-Connected* Call

    Have one person make a phone call and another person pick up the call. The person receiving the call doesn't smile and can pretend to be not too happy to be interrupted and obviously bored with having to inter-act. Maybe the person looks at his/her nails, taps a pencil impatiently, or pretends to sit at a computer screen, playing a game or scanning the Internet while the other person is trying to have a conversation. Wow!

    Now, switch around the roles, letting other persons have their turn at being the goofy one! This is fun; most young people really enjoy being the *bad guy* and play the roles broadly, having a good time!

    After two or three of these *worst case* roles, let everyone practice using the best courtesy, kindness and consideration possible, smiling and being a helpful participant in the phone conversation. After the *worst case* scenarios, this positive approach will be a relief!

    Notice how we can *hear a smile!* Note too, the difference that being fully attentive makes in a person's voice and in the attitude that is transmitted even over a phone! Talk with each other about what you observe.

- Trying to Leave a Message with a Non-Helpful Person

    Another possibility might be to take the role of a person receiving a phone call for someone who's not at home or who can't come to the phone. Play the call recipient role as someone who is not at all helpful! Have some fun seeing just how un-connected and un-helpful each of the role players taking this part can be. Note how difficult it is to even leave a simple message when the other person is not helping!

Let those who care to each take a turn at being the *non-helpful* person.

Now, switch the role playing to *the better way*, receiving a call courteously and being helpful with a message request. From unpleasant and frustrating to pleasant and helpful, the contrast in experiences for all involved is dramatic! It's evident that, even in something as basic as taking a message for someone, it's much more pleasant to work together in courtesy and kindness!

- Yet another possibility for role playing might be pretending to be together visiting (this could be workable for two people or for several). Everyone chats it up except for one person who decides that she or he suddenly needs to play a game, surf the Net or get involved in texting. Notice how uncomfortable and distracting this can be. The rude-playing, distracted person could interject a few lame comments during everyone else's visiting with each other, like "Oh, that's for sure!" (and he doesn't even know what's been said), or maybe "Uh-huh" when asked a question.

  Now switch roles and play this again, letting another person take the rude role!

  Finally, let everyone role play together the *good* version of the visiting scenario. Do this in a thoughtful, involved interaction for a minute or two, thinking of comments to make and questions to ask — enjoying each other without any e-communication interruptions. Notice how happy and satisfied everyone is when connected in courtesy and kindness! E-etiquette is a good thing!

5.

Basic Good Grammar Is A Skill — And A Courtesy!

(And it says a lot about us when we open our mouth to speak!)

"Hey, uh, Dude! Me and you have to uh…you know…go there, man… Umm…Like uh…you know…uh…where's it at?"

"Don't worry; me and Jill know where we're going to."

"Where are you at now?"

"Him and me aren't sure where we're at."

Oh, yikes – painful!

It's very common to hear something like these awkward phrases spoken every day – by young people and by adults.

But, just because they may be used frequently or even by *personalities,* it doesn't make it correct nor does it make it sound good – at all!

And, it certainly doesn't represent who we *are* when we have our words sounding awful!

Badly Used Grammar Creates at Least a Poor First Impression!

There are a lot of people who notice poor grammar, who care about how words are used to communicate and who consider using good grammar and speaking well to be a basic part of knowing *how to act* in a social or business situation!

Fair or *unfair* and like it or not, people do judge us by how we use language!

Someone who uses grammar poorly and puts together their words awkwardly or sloppily – perhaps even does so to appear *cool* – may in actuality be an intelligent person and a nice person to know. But, her or his poor language use just says "uneducated" or "doesn't care" or "way too *cool*" for a lot of situations or for many jobs!

When we use proper grammar and speak well, it presents us as a person who knows what he or she is doing.

Learning how to speak well – how to choose the words we use so they sound smooth and not awkward – is a skill!

And that doesn't mean we are going to *get all formal and stiff,* either! Our language can still show our individuality and have fun, zest, color and interest to it! With *good* grammar, our words just won't distract from who we are and what we want to say!

Basic, good grammar can help open those doors of opportunity we speak about in our *Etiquette of Kindness*. And not knowing how to speak well can keep those doors slammed shut!

Who'd have thought: using good grammar skillfully complements who we are and helps us to create positive opportunities; it's another way to be kind to ourselves!

Besides the benefits to ourselves, trying our best to use good grammar is a courtesy to others: when we speak well, we don't subject other people to plain old ugly-sounding, distracting, thrown-together speech. It shows that we care!

So, good grammar – pleasant, skillful speech – is a natural part of our *Etiquette of Kindness* skills and courtesies!

Give 'em a Test!

Since knowing which words to choose to express what we want to say is not always easy, a handy-dandy thing to remember is to:

> TEST words to see if they are needed to complete the thought or whether they are needed to make sense in our sentence.

It makes it simple!

With our Word Test, no one will know (if we don't want them to) that we're figuring out how to say what we want, right in the moment! Using our little test, it takes just seconds to check or quickly figure out our grammar *on the fly* while we are talking and considering what we want to say!

Taking on Some Common *Grammar Traps* (Tips for getting them right – *without* an English grammar lesson!)

In the following sections, we'll take a look at some common problematic word combos and choices – *grammar traps!*

Formal grammar lessons are great, but they are not what we need for rounding out our *Etiquette of Kindness* skills. For our purposes, we won't be labeling and memorizing parts of speech or remembering all sorts of rules for tenses, etc. We'll take a more casual, easy and very effective approach to increasing our communication and social skills.

We will use simple tools for hearing and seeing what is correct and we'll especially learn how our Word Test can make picking which words to use an easy skill — and a fun one!

And, the beauty is, once we get used to checking our wording — and to getting it right — correct grammatical use and smooth phrases become second nature. Oh, joy and confidence!

When we're done with this chapter, it'll be super simple to get a lot of our daily conversational wording *right on!*

"Him and me…" "Me and her…" "Them and me…" "Her and me…" "Him and you…" "All of us don't know *nothing!*"

Let's get started with a half-dozen commonly heard, awkward and incorrect grammatical choices.

1. *"Him and me* are going now."

2. *"Me and her* don't know for sure."

3. *"Them and me* are out of luck!"

4. *"Her, Jill and me* might go to the movies."

5. *"Him* and you should come meet us."

6. "All together we *don't know nothing!"*

Geez! These all sound pretty goofy — and they certainly need improvement! What to do?

Put the *Other Guy* First!

First *rule:* we put the other person or persons first in our listing of people. *I* or *me* (depending upon what word is called for in our sentence) come last!

Next, Test It!

We then test the sentence to see how it would read or what it would sound like if we left in only one person as the subject for the *action.*

For our first sentence:

1. "Him and me are going now."

   Word Test it by taking everyone out except for just one person...

   "Him is going now?" No: "He is going now."

   "Me am going now?" No: "I am going now."

   So, using our rule of the other person first, let's rewrite that first sentence to read:

   "He and I *are* going now."

   (Since there is more than one person involved in our statement, we of course, use the plural form to express our action: "...*are going."*)

Voilà! Simple!

Let's take the second sentence:

2. "Me and her don't know for sure."

   Test it by taking one person out and seeing how it sounds.

   "Her don't know for sure? No, "She doesn't know for sure."

"Me don't know for sure"? Nope, of course not; "I don't know for sure."

So, when we put the two people together again in our sentence, here's how it needs to be, *using the other person first rule*:

"She and I don't know for sure."

Moving on to our third sentence, let's do the same:

"Them and me are out of luck."

Now, using our Word Test rule…

"Them are out of luck"? No! "They are out of luck."

"Me is out of luck"? Of course it's "I am out of luck."

Fortunately, we are *all in luck* because we now know how to say this! We put the other person or in this case more than one other person first:

"They and I are out of luck."

Okay, we are getting this!

Fine! Next sentence:

3. "Her, Jill and me might go to the movies."

   Wow! Let's get right to this!

   "She might go to the movies."

   "Jill might go to the movies."

   "I might go to the movies."

Put everyone all together going to the movies and it becomes

"She, Jill and I might go to the movies."

Whew! Almost done with our examples – and we're getting this down!

On to our next-to-last example:

4. "Him and you should come meet us."

   This is actually easy! We can say

   "You and he should come meet us."

   Or, not quite as clear or as nice-sounding to the ear, but acceptable,

   "He and you should come meet us."

Double Trouble!

And the final in our Word Test examples:

5. "All together we don't know nothing!"

   Well, that may certainly be the case – it sure sounds like we don't know much if our choice of wording is a clue!

   If what we are saying here is that we just *don't know anything*, or that we *know nothing*, then we simply get rid of that ridiculous *double negative* – combined *don't* and *nothing* – and say it like this:

   "All together we don't know *anything!*"

   Or, if we want to use the word *nothing*, and if we want to make an even sleeker sentence, then we use it properly, like this:

   "All together, we know *nothing!*"

Whew! Much better! (And, obviously, we really do know a great deal as evidenced by our word choices! Yaay, us!)

So, our Word Test is working to make things clearer and clearer, simpler and simpler. We'll continue!

"Good grammar is *where it's at!*"
"I just don't know where verbal expression is going *to!*"

Oh, my! Obviously, even sentences meant to express our heart-felt, sincere concerns can end in goofy-sounding ugliness!

Just like invasive weeds in our speech, that *hanging* *at* and that *tacked-on* *to* — each of which makes no sense and adds nothing to a sentence — are sprouting everywhere today!

Sticking on an unnecessary *at* or *to* at the end of our sentences shows a lack of decisiveness and strength in what we are saying. That's not what we want to convey in our own speech — and not even what we want to hear in others' verbal expression!

Even some high-profile adults and professionals — journalists or news people and interviewers for instance — are now getting into this habit of ending with an unnecessary, weakening and awkward *at* or that silly added *to!*

Possibly, it is an attempt at just sounding *casual*. Whatever the reasoning, it simply clutters up and diminishes the thoughts people are trying to express!

Though we hear *at* and *to* misused in this way all too frequently, it doesn't affect us, because we are on the track of better grammar and of sounding like we know what's what!

Let's move on quickly then to tackle that pesky, misplaced (but easily handled!) *at* hanging out at the end of sentences! Likewise, we'll handle that unnecessary *to*, too — along with some other awkward *grammar traps!*

"Like, uh...*you know*...good grammar's the thing!"

Okay, now! Let's look at the few sentences that started off our chapter here, *Good Grammar Is a Skill – and a Courtesy:*

- "Hey, uh, Dude! Me and you have to uh...you know...*go* there, man... Umm...Like uh...You know...uh...where's it at?"

- "Don't worry; me and Jill know where we're going to."

- "Where are you at now?"

- "Him and me aren't sure where we're at."

We're going to save the amazingly bad first sentence about "Hey, uh, Dude..." to tackle last. So, now that we know what to do with me, you, them, him, her... we'll just get right to that hanging *at* and that added, unnecessary *to* in our sentence:

"Don't worry; me and Jill know where we're going to."

(Or, this could also read just as poorly,

"Don't worry; me and Jill know where we're going *at*.")

The rule here is: If a word isn't needed or if it's just hanging out there, referring back a second time to something already stated, we throw it out of our sentence!

Therefore, using our proper grammar regarding the order of the people referred to in a sentence, this first sentence example we're working with should simply read

"Don't worry; Jill and I know where we are going."

(NO *at* or *to* hanging there at the end, please!)

Now, another example of that pesky *at:*

"Where are you *at* now?"

What we do with this unnecessary *at* is simple — throw it out! This sentence now says, straight to the point

"Where are you now?"

Or, this could read more simply and very much complete in thought —

"Where are you?"

Our third sentence example gives us another chance to practice not only what to do with that silly *hanging at,* but also how to list our friends in our sentences:

"Him and me aren't sure where we are at."

Oh, my! Let's make short work of this —

"He and I aren't sure where we are."

NO need for that ugly *at* hanging out there at the end, of course!

"Of dudes...and umm...like...uh...man...like...*you know*...like...uh...other awkward non-essentials!"

Bringing a number of awkward word choices all together, our *ugly award* for worst sentence of our chapter goes to the *Big Kahuna* example:

"Hey, uh, Dude! Me and you have to uh...*you know*...*go* there, man... Umm...Like uh...You know...uh...where's it at?"

My...my...my, *ugly* from so many angles! Let's pick it apart!

*Uh...umm...*GIVE 'EM A REST!

When we are speaking, not every moment needs to be filled with the sound of our words! Brief pauses can give our speech shape, color and rhythm not heard if we are compulsively filling the air with "Uh...um..."!

Unfortunately, we even have some of our most public, prominent figures scattering their speech liberally with these weakening words! Too bad, because…

Uh and *umm*… are fillers and distracting.

We can take these out of our conversation and just:

Rest in our phrasing and gather our thoughts for a moment, without filling the pause with "Uh…ummm…"

"Hey, *man,* there are a lot of *dudes* out there!"

Most of the time, calling people *dude* just doesn't work well. It's the same thing with *man* as it's used above in our heading and in our *prize-winning-ugly* sample sentence. If we're going to occasionally use one of these words, then we want to consider not overusing these terms by adding another in the same sentence or short paragraph. We certainly don't want to pepper our conversation with frequent use of *dude* or *man*.

Sometimes, people choose to use this *dude* or *man* to cover up that they just don't remember the other person's name!

If we use one of these catch-all, non-specific names to address someone we are just meeting, as in: "Hey, dude (man), glad to meetcha!" we have a very real chance that we won't remember the *actual* name that was used to introduce this new-to-us-person. Using *man* or *dude* in this case is almost a name-forgetting guarantee!

It's far better to repeat the other person's name: "Hey, Sam, glad to meet you!" Our brain will remember *Sam* much better than this guy as *dude* in our long list of *dudes!* Sloppiness in using names makes it easy for us to forget – and to appear careless!

(For more on smooth, effective introductions please see our chapter: *Making Your Acquaintance…*)

And, please: we don't use these names for our mom or dad or for our teachers, or for anyone other than our very closest *peer dudes* – and even then, not *all* the time!

"It's *like — you know...!*"

Using *like* as filler, as is so often heard these days, isn't really saying anything — doesn't add anything, as in: "I was, like, really teed-off!"; or maybe "You know, like really..."; or as in our long, ugly-prize sentence, combined with "...Uh...like..."

In these examples the word *like*:

• Is pure filler

• Distracts from what the person is trying to relate

• Needs to be struck out if we want to be heard at our best!

More *Word Fluff!*

Add *you know* to that misused and unnecessary *like* and we've got some true *throw-aways* doing nothing but taking up mental processes, conversation space and information sharing!

This filler *you know* is used all too often as another way to fill a natural thought-gathering pause with meaningless words.

Many people misuse this phrase repeatedly today as if they couldn't speak (or think) without this word fluff — but the habitual use of filling our conversations with *you know* or with "You know?" unnecessarily weakens what we want to express.

And then we have that *hanging at* there at the end — and we know what to do with that — give it the editing ax!

The nicer, shorter version!

Again, here's our really poor sentence:

> "Hey, uh, Dude! Me and you have to uh...*you know*...*go* there, man... Umm...Like uh...You know...uh...where's it at?"

We can go from that to our shortened, refreshed and refined sentence which could be:

> "Hey, Steve! You and I have to go there! Where is it?"

Or possibly, we take "Hey!" out altogether and make it more *polished*:

"Steve! You and I have to go there! Where is it?"

Or perhaps (but *seldom, please*):

"Hey, man (dude)! You and I have to go there! Where is it?"

We might agree: the person speaking a *cleaned up* version of our sentence sounds like he knows what he's doing and saying – as if he's a lot more educated and capable than when we first heard his words before we correctly pared them down!

Here we are at the end of our basic grammar section – we did it! Not too painful, eh?

Bringing Our Basic Good Grammar All Together – Because We Care!

Let's recap our basics we've learned in our efforts to *be heard* as we desire to present ourselves:

1. Word Test!

> If we're confused about what word to use, we use our Word Test, changing our sentence momentarily in our heads to just a singular subject for the action, to see if taking that word (or words) out makes the sentence read clearly as in:

> "Her, him and me are going to the movies" we quickly test with: "She is going…", "He is going…" and "I am going…"

> So we know that this sentence constructed properly becomes

> "She, he and I are going to the movies."

2. Keep 'em in order!

> When talking about more than ourselves, we always *put the other person/people first* in our listing, so using this knowledge, along with our other skills.

"Me and Jill and her might go" becomes "She, Jill and I might go."

3. NO *at* or *to* hanging out!

If we are using the word *at* near the end of our sentence, or have it hanging out there at the very end, it *garbages up* our idea and we need to give it the axe!

> So, "I don't know where she's at now" becomes just "I don't know where *she is* now." (Or, perhaps: "I don't know where she is.")

> Likewise, "I don't know where she's going at" becomes simply "I don't know where she's going."

Easy! Really simple!

4. NO *like really!*

If we are going to talk about something or someone, we just say it — we don't add *like!*

> "She is *like* really pretty!" is made so much better (shows us off at our best) when we simply say:

> "She is really pretty!"

> Now that's talking about what we think of her — and not cluttering our comment up with the misused and distracting *like!*

5. *Double* trouble!

There is *nothing* wrong with *nothing* when we use that word as it's intended! So, we keep it in its proper place and don't use it as a *double negative:*

> "They don't see nothing" becomes correctly "They see nothing!"

6. *You know…*it's simple!

You know, it's fine to use *you know* — when it's needed!

But when we use it in sentences without any purpose other than to *you know* hold a space while we — *you know* — think, or to somehow oh, *you know* seem *with-it* in a lame sort of way, we dilute our comments and ideas with all of that filler!

If we want our thoughts to be heard, we share what we want to share, straight up and use this phrase only when it's needed and makes sense — as in the very first two words of our first line above, "You know, its…!"

7. Just *say* it!

We keep a lookout in our speech for that habit of *uh, umm…*We realize that it's okay to just pause for a moment if we need to gather our thoughts — and we don't have to fill that split second with *uh* or *umm!*

8. Cluttering it up with *Dude* and *Man!*

These two distracting, cluttering filler-titles, *Dude* and M*an,* can work against any desire we might have to be better heard!

Each of these words should be kept to a minimal, low-level usage, saving either for very casual circumstances — and then not overusing them!

We realize that most adults don't favor being called *Dude* or the like, so we just don't *go there!*

Drum roll, please…We're done!

So, there we have it for some courteous, kindly and clarifying *good grammar basics* — adding yet more skills to the others that we are learning in our *Etiquette of Kindness!* Excellent!

Practice Opportunities:

Have some fun with family and friends! Consider making up your own *Big Kahuna worst-case* sentences and have fun picking them apart. Use grammatically awkward and poorly chosen words and phrases such as: "Um…", "It's like, uh…", "…where it's at", "Her and me…", "Hey, uh, Dude…", or pick from others in our chapter or from those you think up yourself. Take a few minutes to privately write out some really bad sentences, and then take turns sharing and editing until all of your examples of bad grammar are fixed. Be sure to use our Word Test and other grammar hints we've given here to easily make the changes. Enjoy the laughter as you skillfully turn *scream-in-the-night* awful sentences into those of proper grammar!

Try a *Search and Destroy Word Habit Wipe-Out!*

If you'd like to weed out or minimize some particular words or filler sounds that you habitually over-use in expressing yourself, consider devoting a week to that one communication improvement effort. Perhaps, for example, you find yourself using a *lot* of filler "Ummm…" or "Uh…", or perhaps calling *everyone* by the non-name of "Dude" or maybe tacking on that useless "at" as the last word of a sentence.

- Pick one or two of these or other poor speech habits and concentrate on lessening their use when you talk, text or write. Keep your sense of humor as you make your "search and destroy word habit wipe-out" into a game!

- If you care to, go back in this chapter to find any handy hints for alternatives to the words or filler sounds you'd like to change or eliminate.

- Dedicate a week (one hour…one day at a time) to better awareness and practice. You may find you want to extend the period of better self-expression skills you've acquired. You may find that a month would be a fun achievement, and then — who knows!

You'll be proud of your success! You can do this!

6.

Thank You!

Writing Letters and Notes —
Saying "Thanks!" and "Hello!"

Saying "thank you!" — expressing gratitude — is an act of thoughtfulness and it's basic in our Etiquette of Kindness.

When we combine our gratitude to someone with telling them we care about them, we are interested in them and we appreciate them, then saying "thank you" becomes a communication of which we can be proud. This makes us feel good about ourselves!

It's About the Other Person

Saying "thank you!" is more about the other person and the thoughtfulness and generosity shown, than about us!

No matter how we do this — by written note, by a call, by texting, e-mail, or by whatever new-and-improved e-communication that comes along — a sincere thank you in which we have taken time and care is *always* welcomed by others!

Whatever the form we choose to say "thank you!" we always keep in mind the other person who's reading what we write or listening to what we say.

I Is Not the First Word!

Usually, we want to try to *not* start off the first line in our note or comments by using the word *I* as the very first word, as in: "I really like the book you sent me. Thank you"; or "I want to thank you for the sweater you gave me — thanks a lot!"

Of course there are exceptions when we might want to use *I* as the first word. But in general, writing thank-yous and most notes and letters is stronger, more interesting and holds the reader's attention better if we don't put *I* as the first word!

Also, when we communicate our thanks by phone or online, it usually works best if we avoid beginning with *I* but instead start off with the other person and what he or she has done.

This idea of no *I* first and how to make it work, will become clear as we go along with examples.

Interesting, Thoughtful and Timely!

Let's take a look at how we can express our gratitude in writing. We'll learn to make our communications interesting and meaningful!

We'll go over some ways we can be certain that we are up on *when, why, how and to whom* we should say "thank you very much." Here we go!

To whom to say "Thank you!"

Every person considerate of us deserves our thanks!

- We express thanks to anyone who does us a courtesy, hosts us, gives us a gift, etc.

- Relatives should not be forgotten in our thanks just because they are *relatives!* Grandparents, aunts/uncles...all certainly like to feel appreciated. They are proud to see children in their family understand the importance of good manners – and how to use them.

When to say "Thank you!"

Being told "thank you!" is *always* appreciated by the other person!

- We say "thank you!" in a *timely manner* – ideally within 10 days of receipt of a gift or a good deed.

- It is *never too early to say "thank you!"*

- *It is never too late to say "thank you!"*

When we have received a gift package in the mail or via a carrier, say for our birthday or for a holiday, it's always thoughtful and appreciated for us to make a phone call (e-mail or text if the person uses this regularly). We always let the sender know of its arrival, especially if the package is intended to be opened later, on the date of a celebration!

When we've forgotten, or if we find that we've just *messed up* and have put off giving our thanks, we:

- Put aside our likely embarrassment.

- Put the other person's feelings first from this point on.

- Say "thank you!" even if we are late in giving our thanks!

Here is where "better late than never" really holds true!

> We'll see in further detail under *How to say "Thank you!"* that when communicating a late "Thank you!" we can send a note – a handwritten note is always the nicest selection. We could also call or e-mail to tell the person how much we have enjoyed the gift/the memory of the nice thing done for us, etc.

<u>Why</u> to say "Thank you!"

We express gratitude because someone showed us a kindness and because we are a kind, considerate and courteous person!

- We say "thank you!" because the person that gifted us with a present or good deed appreciates knowing that it suited us/brought us pleasure/was helpful/gave us some fun, etc.

- It's a basic responsibility to respond to a kindness — it's part of good, thoughtful communication!

- Communicating our thanks provides an opportunity for the gift-giver to communicate regarding the gift.

When we've received a kindness, we say "thank you!" whether or not we found the gift or deed *suitable* to our situation, needs or desires. We still thank the person for their kindness/generosity/thoughtfulness, etc.

Many people who give us a gift (especially grandparents!) may want to check with us to see if the gift is suitable, what we can use or might like. Thanking the person provides the opportunity for sharing that information. The gift-giver may ask us if the style/color/size/type, etc. is what we really want; they may want to make a change if something could be corrected. We honor their desires to get it right for us. We are honest — all the while expressing appreciation for their concern, generosity, etc.

<u>How</u> to say "Thank you!"

With some very few exceptions, a physical *written note* sent in the mail is correct, preferred and appreciated!

- For many of our purposes of expressing thanks, we can include written notes *along with* other forms of *thanks!*

- Sometimes it is good to initially call/speak to the person — and then follow up soon after with a written note, telling how much the kind gift or gesture has been appreciated.

- If we have occasion to call the person as part of our thank-you, we'll not only express thanks for the gift/kindness, we'll also inquire about the other person; we will help to create an interesting conversation.

- If we reach a message machine when we call, we'll leave a brief message regarding the purpose of our call and then call back later.

- We could write a thank-you initially and follow up later with a call to the person, relating how we've enjoyed the item/loved the memories of the kindness and generosity shown. This is a nice added gesture of our appreciation!

- Depending upon the nature of the kind gesture, in very casual day-to-day circumstances, a phone call or relating our thanks in person can be sufficient.

- Today, some people find it acceptable to communicate thanks via e-mail.

    We use our judgment regarding whether e-mail is the usual/preferred manner for this person, and in that case, we consider also sending an e-card – in which we *personalize* our thanks with an added note.

- Also, with so much use of *texting* and *e-mail* today, another newly acceptable combination of saying "thank you!" would be to text or e-mail the person that we received the gift (in the case of the gift being a package or e-gift sent out to us) and that we'll be writing a mailed note very soon.

    This is *not a replacement for writing and sending a thank-you note!*

    This initial texting/e-mail is just a gesture of courtesy to let someone know that the gift arrived, that we appreciate the thoughtfulness, and that we'll be writing as soon as we've opened the kind remembrance or perhaps utilized the e-gift.

- If we decide to use a purchased greeting card, we not only sign our name, we also:

  > Write a thoughtful, interesting note to the person as well, instead of having our message be merely the commercially-created printed greeting.

  > Follow our guidelines for neatness, gratitude and interest in the other person.

- No matter the form, we always use our best grammar and check spelling.

- When we write that note for mailing, we use our neatest handwriting and balance our sentences and paragraphs so they are visually pleasing on the page. (We won't cram all the writing up at the top of the page, with lots of blank space left below.)

- Using a pen is preferable, and making a rough draft that is then copied is also just fine if it makes us more comfortable.

- If there is *a physical reason* that makes it uncomfortable or not doable to use handwriting for any writing purposes, then we can perhaps use a computer or phone. We follow the same basic ideas we are sharing here regarding showing gratitude. *However* it's accomplished, the main idea is to express our thanks for a courtesy done for us by another.

- Whatever the communication form used, we make it interesting; we express personal wishes for and interest in the other person, for example:

  > "Are you and Grandpa are ready for the big storms I have heard you expect up there this winter? I sure hope so! Keep safe and warm!"

  > Or perhaps, "How was your trip to the Southwest this year? I know you like to go every spring to see the wild flowers."

  > Or, "How's your garden coming this spring? I remember that last year..."

- We want to remember to make every effort to start our note without using *I* as the first word. Begin about *the other person* and what she or he has done! For example:

  "The sweater you gave me is perfect! Thank you for selecting such a great style. I love it…"

  Or, "How did you know I needed help with my costs for books for college this year! You are always so thoughtful!"

  Or perhaps, "Getting your package was such a nice surprise — and reminded me of how much I miss seeing you in person."

- We use care with the envelope, making it neat and clear (see below, *Addressing Envelopes*).

- If we call to say "Thank you!" then it is *always* appreciated that we write an additional follow-up thank-you a bit later telling the person how much we are enjoying the gift!

  This could be, for instance, about what we did with the gift money; how much we liked wearing the jacket; how terrific the book was…

  Writing the additional note goes beyond simple recognition of any gift. It also shows a depth of caring, appreciation and attention to our friendship/relationship.

What if…?

If we are given something that just doesn't work for us — something we really don't like or can't use:

- We can always focus our thanks on some aspect of the gift itself — *and* on the kindness, thoughtfulness, generosity and the time it took to select or make the gift.

- We can say "thank you!" sincerely and with the same format of interest and kindness that we use in all of our communications.

If our friend or relative asks us "Does it fit?", "Can you use it?" "Was that the one you were looking for?" and is asking us for information so they can change the gift in some way to make it better for us:

- We should honestly give them the information they are requesting! In this case, they really want to know so they can do something different, and it's kind to help them — while thanking them for their thoughtfulness in the original gift, *and* now in wanting to make it even nicer/more suitable or useable.

    > Example: *Aunt Mary* gives us a lime green ski jacket and we look awful in lime green — what do we do? We handle it gracefully and gratefully. We thank Aunt Mary for her thoughtfulness and generosity and perhaps comment on the great styling of the jacket. If our aunt wants to check further to see if the jacket is really suitable or what we like, we can converse with her honestly, kindly and sensitively, honoring the fact that she wants to *get it right* for us!

- If we've already sent a note or called in thanks for the original gift, then, after an additional effort has been made to change the gift in some way, we will write or call *again*. We will thank them for their added kindness and efforts on our behalf — and report on how great the gift now is!

- And if, as we said earlier here, we procrastinate or forget to give our thanks, we will waste no more time with writing a note or picking up the phone to do the correct thing — finally! No matter when, an expression of thanks for thoughtfulness given is always appreciated and always a good thing!

Addressing Envelopes

Addressing envelopes so that they have the best chance to reach their desired destination is not difficult!

The post office likes to use a simple, clear format:

- The return address (name may/may not be included here — your choice) goes in the upper left hand corner on the front (not on the back flap anymore, with the possible exception being in very formal situations such as wedding invitations); the stamp is put in the upper right corner.

- The name and address of the person/entity to whom you are mailing your letter goes in the middle of the envelope.

- The post office prefers block printing, not cursive, and no periods or commas between the town/city and the state, or between the state and the zip code. In other words, *no punctuation at all* when addressing envelopes!

Your Name (or not)
1111 Your Street (or P.O. Box 123)
Your Town MA 23456

Addressee (If appropriate, use Mr./Mrs./Miss/Ms or company name)
333 Their Street (or P.O. Box #) (add Apt. #, if applicable)
Their City WA 98765 (all on one line - no commas or periods)

- Personal notes and thank you's should always be hand-addressed directly on the envelope, and in ink. Using mechanical printing (computer or typewriter) to address an envelope should be reserved for business use.

Let's Recap and Consider Further!
Writing casual notes and thank you's can be fun!

The communication of gratitude and/or friendship can be enjoyable and fulfilling when

- We remember to focus on the persons to whom we are writing, on making it a lot about them, their interests and/or their kindness toward us.

- We are sincere and friendly! We can almost be assured that other people will find our notes interesting, kindly and gracious – and a pleasure to read when we take this approach.

- We use this same spirit of friendliness and sincerity for our conversations in e-mail, texting or by phone, as we've covered in other sections of *The Etiquette of Kindness.*

Now, on to some more points about *form* in our writing.

Beginning Without *I!*

As we've said, we try most times to *not begin our notes with the word I,* using instead our creativity and our interest in the other person(s) to spark our writing of an interesting, friendly communication!

Of course, there are exceptions as, for instance, the note below in our samples – the one of condolence from *Matthew,* where he elected to begin with "I..." to start saying how personally very sorry he was for what had occurred. In this example, it worked just fine to begin with "I..." Usually, however, we try to stretch our writing and communication skills by finding other ways to begin our notes and letters!

Certainly, practicing this approach of beginning our comments centered not on "I...", but on the person to whom we are writing, takes extra effort! But ultimately, it helps us to write a more interesting note as we think more creatively and deeply about what we are going to say!

Dates are Good!

Usually, we put a date in the upper right-hand portion of our note. (Less frequently, it's written in the top middle of the note.)

Let's take a look at some common-use examples of noting the date, going from the most casual (just the day of the week) to the more formal ways of indicating days or dates:

- For very casual use, we could simply spell out the day of the week
    Tuesday (or whichever day)
- We could add the spelled-out month and numerical day as well
    Tuesday, April 27th _
- Also, we could remove the spelled-out day and enter our date this way
    April 27th

- We could also indicate our date with abbreviations
  Tues., Apr. 27, '10 or Apr. 27, '10
- We can spell out the day of the week, as well as the month, and use numbers to show the count of the day and of the year
  Tuesday, April 27, 2010
- We can use all numbers for our date, separating day-month-year either by a hyphen or a forward slash
  4-27-2010 or 4/27/2010
  (Or 4-27-10 or 4/27/10)
- We could combine spelling out the day of the week along with a numerical date, probably stacking the day and the date
  Tuesday
  4-27-2010
- For noting the date more formally, we don't add a spelled-out day of the week, instead we do spell out the month
  April 27, 2010
  (Note: if we are ever in doubt, this format can be used for nearly every correspondence application. It's always correct.)
- And, though there'll be relatively rare occasions to use the next style, just for fun and for our knowledge, let's spell out every aspect of this date
  April twenty-seventh, two thousand and ten
  (Variations of this form are used for very formal social and legal applications, such as for wedding invitations and legal documents)

Whew! Those are a lot of possibilities! But, here's the good news: most of our day-to-day communications are fairly casual, allowing us to be pretty flexible in picking which date formats to use.

Spelling and Grammar DO Count!

Whether writing by hand (with a pen, if possible please, or with an unsmeared pencil in our best, clearest, neatest handwriting) or on a computer, phone, tablet or other device, we take care to spell correctly; we use the good grammar we are learning.

Certainly, texting is handy, but it has gotten us into the habit of using phonetic abbreviations as speedy shortcuts for casual communications. This can make it difficult to remember how to spell words out when we need to do that!

When we are writing a nice note, spelling correctly and paying attention to creating our phrases well and pleasingly say *I care*; that I have the ability to think and to transmit my thoughts to others respectfully and thoroughly.

Taking a few extra seconds to text in the same manner keeps us remembering how to spell and exercises and sharpens our creative and social mind! Making texting abbreviations the exception and good-grammar, well-spelled texts the norm would go a long way in keeping us skillful communicators!

If it hasn't already been read – or if there are any questions of our falling into common *poor grammar traps* – a helpful idea might be to go to our chapter 5, *Basic Good Grammar Is a Skill – and a Courtesy! (And, it says a lot about us when we open our mouth to speak!)*

In that chapter, we share some common grammar traps and have more handy hints to help make getting grammar right, a doable simple thing! In *Basic Good Grammar is a Skill – and a Courtesy,* we find some easy, super-quick mental tools – *word tests* – to which we can immediately turn for a second, even in mid-conversation! With those word test tools, we will seem to be word-usage champs!

We Are "at" Nowhere (without Good Grammar and Spelling)!

As with chapter 5, *Basic Good Grammar is a Skill – and a Courtesy,* this section is also *not* an English grammar lesson, using parts-of-speech labeling and memorization or remembering all sorts of rules for tenses, etc!

For our purposes in our note, thank-you and letter writing conversation here, we'll remember the basics of some all-too-common grammar usage challenges we see and hear so often today.

We consider each common challenge to good grammar individually and simply, so let's take them from the top!

<u>"We can begin where we're *at!*"</u>(Sigh!)

We remember that, if we want to know where someone is, we say "Where are you?" We don't say, "Where are you *at?*" The phrase "Where are you?" is complete. Adding "at" is just sloppy, *not cool*, sounds rather goofy, and it's really poor grammar; it adds no information and means nothing at all!

Likewise, statements such as "This is where I am." or, "This is where they are," or "This is where she is." are complete statements as they stand!

We don't tack "at" on the end of any question or statement regarding location!

<u>"We know where we're going *to!*"</u> (Oh, my!)

Well, we do know where we are going grammatically *if* we know *not* to attach that unnecessary, awkward and uglifying "to" at the end of our sentence!

"We know where we're going" is a complete thought.

So, we don't add "to" at the end of our sentence or question! It adds nothing – and it's distracting when we tack that on, as it points out a lack in good grammar usage – something we *don't* want to convey!

<u>"It's great that you're writing your note!"</u>

We sometimes mix up *you're*, as in the contraction form of "You are here." and *your*, as in "This is your note."

Even helpful tools, such as *Spell Check,* often fail to *get* what we are trying to say and insist on our changing a *your,* into *you're* when it should be *your*.

So, if we care to make our spelling and grammar right, we really just have to know what is correct – no matter what any tricky spell-checker may say! We can't leave good grammar usage that expresses what *we* want to say up to chance or automation.

Let's take a good, simple look at correct usage of *you're* and *your*:

> "*You're* going to the store with *your* wallet."

> "*Your* heart is so big and *you're* always thinking of others!"

Your shows possession (*your* wallet or *your* heart) and *you're* (*you're* going or *you're* always) is a contraction or a shorter way of saying *you are* – simple!

It doesn't hurt to note here that when we *say* the word *you're,* since it's a contraction of *you are,* it is pronounced differently from *your. You're* is said: *yoo'rr,* while *your* is pronounced as *yor.* So, if we tend to hear and say the spoken difference, it's possible we'll get our written versions of these words correctly spelled for our intended use!

"It's good that the bird found its nest!"

Here are two other often-misused words, spelled the same, except for that helpful (but sometimes pesky!) apostrophe:

> *it's* as in *it's* good

> and

> *its* as in the bird found *its* nest!

Here is the nitty-gritty on IT'S/ITS:

It's is the shortened version – the contraction – for *it is.* In our sample sentence then, *it's* is the contraction for "*It is* good that the bird…!"

Here are some more examples of choosing to use *it's,* rather than the longer, *it is:*

> *It's* about time.

> We know *it's* true.

> Maybe *it's* gold!

> *It's* the contraction!

Now, continuing…

<u>Its</u> – just plain, with no apostrophe – shows possession, as in the example we gave above: "It's good that the bird found *its nest.*" We don't fancy it up with an apostrophe!

This is sort of tricky, because we might find ourselves wanting to add an apostrophe to show possession of its nest by the bird – but we don't do that here or in any other similar cases:

The boat slipped its moorings.

Some dog lost its collar.

My shirt lost its button.

The sun cast its glow.

(Note: The use of *it's* and *its,* is another case where WORD'S *Spell Check* may ask us to make an incorrect change – but we're on to its occasional mistakes! We won't change our choice of words when we know what we mean and that we're using *it's* and *its* correctly.)

"<u>Their</u> they go again; <u>there</u> getting <u>they're</u> words all mixed up!" (Oops!)

Confusion with *there/they're/their* doesn't show up in speaking, because those words all sound phonetically about the same. (If we're saying *they're* with the proper inflection, we will hear the small difference between that word and the less modulated, flatter sounding *their* or *there*, but it's easy to miss that fine point!) It's in the writing of these words that we get into trouble with picking the correct spelling for what we are meaning to say!

Let's take a minute to clear this up simply! Look at our first funny sentence from the heading above:

"<u>Their</u> they go again; <u>there</u> getting <u>they're</u> words all mixed up!"

This should be corrected to read:

"<u>There</u> they go again; <u>they're</u> getting <u>their</u> words all mixed up!"

There

As we use it correctly here in our sentence (*"There* they go…"), *there* shows *direction* indicated or pointed out, as in "The ball rolled over *there."*

They're

Let's go on to *they're* from our sentence: "…*they're* getting…" If we're reading it aloud and if we pronounce it correctly, *they're* has a subtle spoken difference from *there* and *their,* but it's close enough sounding to the other two to bring confusion, so we often just throw it into the bag with the other similar-sounding words!

But:

> *they're* is the shortened form of *they are* – a contraction of *they are* – so that's why we spell it as we do at that point in our sentence, using the apostrophe to indicate that two words have been combined and short- ened for convenience; "…they're getting…" = "…*they are* getting…"

Their

Of course, *their* is the spelling for showing possession or ownership, as in our sentence above, "…getting *their* words all mixed up" or in: "…*their* ball rolled…"

We Might Give Our Location!

In our notes and letters, sometimes we will want to put our return address inside, written on our note or letter. For our casual purposes, we'll usually write our address over the date in the upper right-hand area of our note or letter.

There are more formal ways to add our address to what we are writing when we have formal stationery, for instance, with our name and address pre-printed up at the top-middle of the stationery sheet. But for our regular needs, we can include our return address on our note as below. Please note that, in the body of a letter or note we *do* use a comma after the town/city name, whereas in addressing envelopes, we leave all punctuation out.

3434 Oakmont Ave.
Our Town, WA 99802

January 16, 2011

Dear _____,

Sample Ways to Say "Thank you!" or to Write Casual Notes

Okay, then! Here we go with some samples of interesting, kindly notes that could be written by young people of varying ages and situations. We'll have our own ideas when it comes time to write our personal communications, but this can help get us started!

————•————

July 9, '_ _

Hello, Aunt Jennifer!

Thank you for always saving such great outfits from my cousins for me! Last time, you sent along that cute black fuzzy jacket – I love it! I also really liked those orange and pink shorts with the matching top – very cool! They looked really good with my sandals Dad bought me. Thanks for everything!

Mom and Dad say "Hi!" and that we are going over to your house next week – that will be fun! (We'll bring *Benny* to play at the beach with your dogs.) Mom's bringing her special cupcakes!

Have a good week and see you all soon!

Love you – and thanks again!

Alisha

————•————

Saturday

Hello, Grammy!

You are just terrific! (But, you already know I think that! Hah-hah!)

How did you guess that I was wishing for a red jacket? And, I really like the styling – and that it's waterproof for our cold, rainy winters up here! It fits great, too, with just enough room for me to grow this winter. (Mom says she can't believe how fast Katherine and I are growing!) Thank you so very much, Grammy!

When I talked to you and Grandpa last time, he was feeling pretty bad with the flu. Did he get all over it yet? I sure hope so – and that you didn't get it from him, too!

We are coming down pretty soon – maybe next month – and I can hardly wait to see you again! Let's go out to that taco stand we always love – Roberto's, I think it is – okay?

Thanks again, Grammy, for that great jacket – I love it!

Hug Grandpa for me – and see you both soon! Text me next week, o.k.? ;-)

Love and xx's oo's –

Julianna

Nov. 20, _ _ _ _

Dear Mrs. Gilroy,

There's no way that I could have made all the soccer practices without your kindly taking me! Thank you so much for picking me up along with Elliot, each practice day – and, for always including me in the snacks you brought along so we'd have a better practice. That really helped!

Also, thanks for all the times you helped me and my family out by taking me home from practice when mom couldn't get away from work in time – that helped so much, too!

Next year, I'll be able to drive and then, if there's ever anything with which I could help you, please always remember that I will do anything to help you out – just let me know.

Thanks again, Mrs. Gilroy, for your thoughtful help!

Have a great summer vacation!

Sincerely,

James

Tuesday

Dear Mr. and Mrs. Williams,

If you hadn't taken care of my bird, I don't know how our family could have gone on vacation!

Thank you so much for taking *Tweetster* and feeding and caring for him so well while we were gone for two weeks. He seemed happy with you!

These chocolate chip cookies are the ones that my brother, Wes, and I make pretty often and I wanted to say "thanks!" by bringing you some, too. So, thank you again for helping me – and *Tweetster!*

Your neighbor and friend –

Tay

January 15, _ _ _ _

Dear Aunt Elise and Uncle George –

Your kindness toward me and my family is always so wonderful!

I know Mom called you to say it had arrived, but maybe she didn't tell you that when that big package came before Christmas, it made a lot of excitement in our house! We all knew that there were thoughtful remembrances for each of us in that box!

You made our Christmas morning even nicer – thank you for everything you sent! I'm sure my brothers will be writing to you, but I want to thank you for my gift. How did you remember that I really wanted those last two books in the series I love? Thank you! I started reading the next one the day I got it and am half way through. It's just as good as all the rest and I am eager to read the next one you gave me!

Dad said you are going to be coming out here next summer. Oh, that will be sooo... great! If you can come also for my ninth grade play in the spring, that would be terrific, but if that's not possible, anytime we get to see you will be wonderful! When you do come, I want to share a couple of special fishing spots down on the river with you both – I know how you and I share the love of fishing!

Until I see you, please take care – and know that I love you always and that I will be enjoying those books. Thank you again!

Big hugs to you both –

Alexa

P.S.: Please send me your e-mail address. Here's mine: _____@_____.

7-11-_ _

Dear Sophia –

How are you? I keep thinking of you and wondering how your viola recital went. I know how hard you practiced and for sooo...many long hours every day for months! I hope you "wowed" them and that everyone gave you a standing ovation! (Hah-hah, but seriously!)

I keep practicing my drums and I think I'm getting better, but I'm not sure my family thinks so – LOL! But, my band teacher says I'm doing fine, so I'll keep practicing, too! Besides, I just looovve my drums, you know! I can hardly wait until mom says I can join that band John and James started! Maybe soon, as long as I keep up my grades!

I miss you! I wish we still lived next door to each other like we did! You're tooo...far, now!

Did you ever get a cell phone for your birthday as you thought you would? I got one for Christmas and here's my number: ___-___-____ Call me/text me!

Love you! Byeee!

Katherine

3434 Oakmont Ave.
Our Town, WA 99802
Thursday, April 20, _ _ _ _

Dear Mrs. Connolly –

You are the very best teacher I could ever have! You are my favorite ever!

Thank you so much for teaching me all that you do – and for all of your hard work, love and care you give to me and to the rest of my class...We all love you!

Pretty soon school will be over for this year. I will miss you over the summer, but have a good time with your family – especially if you go to Yosemite!

Next year we are in sixth grade – can you believe it!

My mom and dad say "Hi!" to you and Mr. Connolly.

Your friend forever –

Love,

John

September 17, _ _ _ _

Dear Mr. and Mrs. Anderson –

I was so sad to hear about your beloved old dog, *Sadie*, passing! That was just terrible that she got out and got hit by a car! My mom and dad always say that people drive too fast on our road, and there you go – poor Sadie got hit!

Again, I am so sorry for the sadness you must feel…I will miss seeing her on my way to school. She was pretty and a good, friendly dog and I really liked her!

Sincerely, your friend and neighbor –

Matthew

May 3, _ _ _ _

Dear Aunt Janet,

It doesn't seem like it's been three months since you gave me my darling kitten! When you gave *Sugar Paws* to me, it was the happiest day of my life!

I'm sorry I haven't written before now (I meant to), but I really do love her – and thank you so much for giving her to me! She was the best gift ever! Having her to play with and take care of every day (she sleeps with me, too!) has made my life so much happier!

I can't thank you enough, Aunt Janet! I've taken some pictures (enclosed here) so you see how well I take care of her and how *Sugar Paws* has grown – isn't she pretty? Doesn't she have the prettiest eyes ever? I love her little white feet!

Did you end up keeping any of the kittens? Didn't her mommy have five?

Mom said you and Uncle Jerry are coming to see us this summer – I can hardly wait, and I get to show you how wonderful "our" little kitty is then!

I love you and I thank you every day in my heart when I hug my darling little S.P.!

See you soon!

XXX, OOO –

Emily

12/15/_ _

Hi, Grandpa!

Thanks so much for coming to my play! I loved that you were there! It was pretty funny, wasn't it?

I liked playing my part of St. Michael and the dragon. My costume was cool. Mom spent a lot of time making it for me!

Please come see us again really soon – I love you and miss you!

I'll call you soon!

Love,

Michael

November 30, '_ _

Dear Aunt Mary –

You are so thoughtful!

Thank you for suggesting that I might want a different color in that great jacket you sent to me – and for including the receipt! I really appreciate that!

As it turns out, since it was early enough in the ski season, they did have another color that I like better on me than lime green...I found a sort of turquoise blue that I really like – same style, too! I think you'd like it on me, also, Aunt Mary!

Do you think you will be able to see any of our Jr. High snow board team in competition up here this year? Coach says I'm doing well and I'd sure like for you to make a competition, if you could. Besides, you could see me in person that way, in that great board jacket you bought me! Hah-hah!

Are you skiing anymore? Was it in Utah last year that you had that ski accident? I sure hope you still get to ski and that your broken ankle is no longer giving you any problems! I was so sorry that happened to you – ouch!

I hope to see you this winter!

I love you and I sure thank you again for my jacket – it's terrific!

Hugs!

Suzy

Saturday

Dearest Julianna –

Thank you for the huge box of books! It's a book overload! I hope I get to see you soon. Tell everyone that I said hi.

Love,

Alisha

———◆———

So, there we have them – some interestingly-written sample notes of thanks, condolence and "Hi! How are you?"

The last note in our little gallery was written by an eight-year-old to her eleven-year-old cousin. Short and sweet, in two lines, it holds all the basic facets of thanks, interest and talking about the other person. It even has the always-welcome element of humor! Complete with handmade drawings in the original note, it was evident that a lot of care was taken in simply saying "Thank you!"

All of our sample notes are as much about the other person as about the writer! All of them are good attempts at interesting comments or news that could go on to create more communication in the future. All of them are cordial and kindly. With one exception, which works just fine, all notes begin without using the old cliché of starting the note with *I!*

And each note, whether an actual "thank you!" note or not, is written with elements of gratitude, respect and appreciation!

As with all of our *Etiquette of Kindness* skills we are learning, our note, letter and thank-you writing gives us opportunities for fun, satisfaction and enjoyment. Our communication successes add to our good feelings of confidence, graciousness and accomplishment. Terrific!

Practice Opportunities:

Consider whether there's anyone to whom you owe a note of thanks or a "Hello! How are you?" Also, think if there anyone you know who would be delighted to receive a correspondence from you — for no reason, other than "just because I care!"

Using our hints regarding writing interesting and satisfying letters and notes, write several notes of thanks or hello and mail them out via the post office. This won't take long and Grandma, your cousin, aunt, uncle, grandpa or good friend will be delighted with your offering of thoughtful, carefully-crafted correspondence!

7.

An Attitude of Gratitude!

The Magic of Living in Thankfulness
(And the Antidote to "I'm bored"!)

Joy is a wonderful thing.

It can be *infectious* turning our lives into daily experiences of deep happiness, peace, satisfaction and kindness.

One of the main ways to bring joy into our lives is to have an *attitude of gratitude* – to daily find and name small and large things for which to be grateful, beginning with our first wakefulness in the morning, then continuing during our day and right on through our last moments before sleep!

Whenever we feel lackluster and *bored*, an instant antidote to boredom is to turn our attention to gratitude. Boredom flees in the face of gratitude!

The healing and instant refreshment properties of gratitude can be *magical*, giving new life and *elasticity* to our brains and creating happy moments that build good days.

Gratitude is *energizing!*

Our Glass: Half Empty or Half Full?

When we are thinking negatively and narrowly – without gratitude – our heart, mind and body reflect this. In this frame of mind, we can see a simple drinking glass filled to half-way, and our perception is that it's half-*empty!*

With a negative attitude, we tend to think with restrictions. In this mindset, "No!" is often our response to ideas, limiting our brain's free exploration of possibilities and creative options!

Our hearts are not open to wonderful, positive associations and opportunities when we are thinking, acting and living in negativity and lack.

Our body shows the negativity as well. It mirrors our sense of dejection and hopelessness in our sour facial expression, our hanging head and our shuffling walk. When we are thinking negatively, we also tend to take poor care of ourselves, perhaps eating too little or too much, staying inside in isolation and avoiding exercise.

However! When we decide, even in the moment, to *think and act out of gratitude*, our sense of ourselves, of other people and of our experiences changes dramatically to the positive. Even that drinking glass that we formerly considered to be half-empty becomes for us half-*full!*

With gratitude, we can think more widely and creatively. As "Yes!" becomes our attitude, options come to us more readily and with a sense of possibility and opportunity!

Our associations with people can lighten and improve as our heart opens in gratitude; we find ourselves attracted to other positive, engaged people – and they to us!

Our body reflects our gratitude. We find ourselves smiling, our posture is straighter and our walk peppier. With gratitude, even our appreciation of Nature is revived, and we may find we *need* to be out-of-doors, getting exercise and breathing fresh air. With an *attitude of gratitude*, we often find that we are simply taking better care of ourselves, getting more rest and gratefully enjoying a bounty of fresh, healthful foods in appropriate portions for our health.

Whether we consider ourselves an introvert or an extrovert; whether we are quiet and shy or outgoing and brimming with confidence – *gratitude* has the power to make our life far better!

And gratitude, it turns out, is the basis for living our lives in the *Etiquette of Kindness*! (Who knew?)

Let's get started discovering more wonders about the energizing *magic* of gratitude!

Magical Moments

Everyone can easily find gratitude for the simplest and the most profound things.

We feel grateful for a drink of water to quench our thirst and for a deep life-giving breath; for the sun's rising in the morning and for the breezes cooling our face; for the warmth of summer and for the moon's coaxing plants from the soil; for the renewing rain and chilling snow wetting our head and watering the earth.

We can be inspired to gratitude by the scents of roses and jasmine, mint, strawberries and mangoes; by the intoxicating smells of baking brownies, hot popcorn, brewing coffee and cinnamon rolls right from the oven.

We can realize thankfulness for the happy yelp and tail-wagging greeting of a beloved dog; for the peaceful purr of a contented cat and for the chirps and trilling of birds on the wing.

Gratitude opportunities are everywhere and we have them in abundance!

We experience delight and gratitude when someone puts an arm around our shoulders or gives us a smile when we really need one. We are thankful for the joy of shared laughter and outright gut-hurting, side-splitting hilarity.

Whether it's rain on the roof, the snap of a carrot or (even) our baby brother's ear-splitting yell, we have so many reasons for *thanks*-giving! (Aren't we glad our little brother is healthy enough to scream so lustily?)

Gratitude...gratitude...gratitude...for living this very moment right here and right now — right where we are standing or sitting or lying.

Gratitude Makes the Good Things Better!

Profound thankfulness can make the paths we take in Life and the people we meet along the way more meaningful to us — more vital.

From our biggest questions about the way Life works through our deepest spiritual, religious or philosophical considerations, an open, grateful heart and a mind turned repeatedly in thanks-giving can aid us in any of our quests for clarity, peace, understanding and joy!

An attitude of gratitude certainly helps us to find balance, health, pleasure and value in our daily activities and relationships. In our interactions with casual acquaintances and our dearest friends and family members, gratitude works its magic!

Gratitude for our best friend is a wonderful thing! We experience gratitude for this person whom we tend to take for granted, but without whom our days just wouldn't hold the fun, anticipation and promise, strength, companionship and hope that are present with him or her in our life. Our *attitude of gratitude* helps us to be strong, upright and courageous for our friend, so that we are present when needed, through thick and through thin!

Deep gratitude is certainly in order for the home we enjoy with its security and far-reaching benefits to our health, development, growth and life; with the companionships, experiences and fun that it provides.

Living together in a family can be a wonderful thing — and always comes with small and large challenges, too! For those of us who are blessed with a family who loves us and is *there* for us through thick and thin (whether or not we think they always get their treatment of us *just right*), gratitude and a thankful heart can bring us even greater joy.

Gratitude in our thoughts and actions toward our family often helps to heal and transform, in our perceptions or in actuality, those irritating little details and larger challenges of family life. With the refreshing *attitude of gratitude*, everything can change, as nothing is "fixed" – except abiding love!

Since with gratitude we tend to stand a little taller, sit a little straighter, think a little clearer, act a little nicer and make choices for greater health of body and mind, we also find that we have greater *courage!* With gratitude, we have courage to tackle good things that we might otherwise find daunting and from which we might shrink in avoidance due to their difficulty.

With the positive energy of gratitude we have the courage to try and to reach out, to see and envision! With the *energizing courage* that springs from our *attitude of gratitude* we can hear ourselves saying "Oh, yes! Thank you!" to both positive options and necessary challenges alike.

Our daily opportunities for education are huge reasons for thankfulness. We treasure the abilities to read and to write, to count and figure and to gain practical knowledge for our lives. We find education both in school and out, formally and casually. No matter how and where we learn, we express gratitude for the many good and generous people who come into our life, staying for a while or for a long time, teaching us treasured lessons and Life skills.

We find that with this *attitude of gratitude*, we are spurred by curiosity and by the love of learning to dig deeper, to seek wider in our quests for knowledge and understanding!

We realize that we value excellence in our own education and in those who help us and inform us. With gratitude, education in all of the formal and informal ways it's available to us and the intellectual and practical skills we gain, become alive, vital, energized!

With gratitude, there are no limits to what we can learn, what we can achieve! With a grateful heart, we find ways to learn and do what we need and want — and gratitude is the key to open doors for us!

We Take Nothing for Granted

The ears to hear, the eyes to see, the hands to grip and the legs to walk are marvels for which most of us can give thanks. When we don't have these and other valued physical faculties, or when they are taken from us through accident or illness, we *can* find ways to be grateful in the moment!

There are many people right around us who have gone through extreme challenges and who still find small and large things for which to be grateful. These people shine for us as examples of living a life of gratitude with all its transforming and reviving aspects!

Gratitude Puts the Rough Stuff and the Small Stuff In Perspective!

We have probably felt this ourselves: the healing, transforming nature of gratefulness is mighty! It can take us through the toughest times in Life, helping us to come out on the other side, often filled with a renewed and joyful heart. With humble gratitude, the rough experiences can become surprising, powerful markers of insight and growth in our lives.

More often than we'd like, it's the little daily irritations that throw us off kilter however, that take us out of graciousness and into anger and ugliness. It doesn't have to be that way. We don't have to react badly to small inconveniences or disappointments!

Most of us have been around a few people who are sincerely — and pretty much constantly — *positive,* who seem able to keep nearly every incident in a perspective of equilibrium and who just don't "sweat the small stuff". They seem to know that when it comes to the daily irritations and minor challenges of Life, as someone once said (or maybe it's just a bumper sticker that rings true), "It's nearly all *small stuff*"! People who seem to be able to take Life's "oops!" in stride can be a pleasure to be around.

Our *attitude of gratitude* helps us to be positive and discerning — and more likely to keep things in perspective as we sort out the rough stuff from the small stuff in Life — finding good, constructive ways to handle it all!

Learned or *Natural,* It's Common to Most Happy People

Not all of us, of course, are *wired* to be fairly constantly cheery and nearly always naturally positive. Everyone has varying proportions of many talents, strengths and weaknesses.

People may be especially endowed with strengths such as steadfastness, thoughtfulness and deliberation or perhaps keen organization, tremendous will-forces and insightful brilliance. Abiding and stable quietness, deep and seemingly unfailing kindness, astounding bravery, keen humor and ready wit are other strengths that people have in varying degrees.

And Life itself, of course, is a variety of origins and environments, attitudes and opportunities, hurdles and tasks. Everyone has life advantages and challenges that are at least somewhat different from the next person's.

But, for most happy people, there's a common element that runs through their lives. Whether they lead very simple or super-complex lives, whether they are rich or poor or somewhere in the middle, and whether they face huge challenges or smaller ones, most happy people make an *attitude of gratitude* — thankfulness for the tiniest to the mightiest of things in everyday life — central to who they are.

This transforming attitude can come about either through inborn positivity or through a decision to turn our minds and our habit-patterns of thinking and reacting to the positive — in gratitude!

Both approaches to positivity and gratefulness — either *natural or decided* — still come out with life-enhancing results, hour by hour, day by day!

Boredom Can't Live Here!

And, for most of these people whom we would consider *happy* and who most likely would consider themselves so, too, *boredom* is virtually unknown and rarely experienced!

<u>Try a small exercise</u>: If ever we find ourselves thinking or complaining "I'm *sooo* bored," we can take the next several minutes and begin thinking "Gratitude!" We start perhaps with being grateful for our breath and we pay attention to that for a few seconds. Next, we think for instance, about our eyes or our hands or our feet and legs and we are thankful for however well – or even haltingly – they work for us.

We keep practicing gratitude. We take *gratitude breaks* throughout our day, five minutes here, two minutes there. We think, for instance, "I am grateful for this moment, for the movement of my lungs as I breathe," and we can *be with* that gratitude. We'll be amazed at how true gratitude, even for the most basic things in Life, can *brighten* our attitude and *transform* our moments and days!

Simple gratitude can flip a switch of positive change! When we turn our attention *outward*, going from the pinched, restricted view that is boredom to the many possibilities available with *gratitude*, everything opens up. We are *energized* and *interested!* We are ready to be surprised, delighted, engaged with possibilities – and so *not* bored!

We can lift our own spirits, renew ourselves and find new happiness and contentment immediately! Boredom just doesn't co-exist with all of the good stuff that gratitude naturally brings!

The Really *Big* Thing!

And, here's the Really Big Thing: when we turn our attention, in thankfulness, *outward,* our natural tendency is to *act* in greater kindness and generosity of spirit!

Our immediate world becomes a truly kinder, more peaceful and nicer place. Our actions of gratitude and kindness spread out, one person and one experience to another, on and on, like the ripples on the lake, to people and places we don't even know, until our wider world reflects greater kindness, gratitude and positive opportunities. Fantastic! Nothing gets any better than this!

So now, let's recap the wonderfulness of gratitude!

With an *attitude of gratitude* we can:

- realize new, sometimes instant ideas of brilliance and creativity;

- revitalize our directions and relationships and find new insights into our decisions;

- find fun and adventure in gratitude's path because Life "magic" happens with an open and grateful heart;

- *live joyfully;*

- *be* the positive pebble in the pond, creating ever-widening ripples of goodness and gratitude!

Gratitude just works wonders!

And as it turns out, since a thankful heart and mind prompt kind actions and open doors for us and for others in our lives – drum roll here, please! – An Attitude of Gratitude is *the basis* of the Etiquette of Kindness! Oh, yes!

Discussion (and Practice) Opportunities:

- Go back to the section in this chapter captioned *Boredom Can't Live Here!* Take a look at the exercise suggested regarding using gratitude to turn off boredom – and to simply enhance Life. Practice it, beginning today, this hour! This simple-seeming gratitude exercise can have a huge effect!

- Exchange *gratitude experiences* with family and friends. Take turns in relating your experiences with the ways adopting *an attitude of gratitude* has changed your life experiences or your relationships with others.

For inspiration, perhaps look back in this chapter at the sections: *Gratitude Makes the Good Things Better* and *Gratitude Puts the Rough Stuff and the Small Stuff in Perspective.*

Also, consider how having taken an approach from the standpoint of gratitude *might have* changed an experience for the better, had you known then, what you know now. Consider how, if you could have a "do-over," you might do it differently today, taking an *attitude of gratitude*, positive approach!

Remember to practice our good communications hints, taking care to listen well to others, ask questions and be respectful.

And, this is very important to remember: our sharing of thoughts or experiences is always a private thing, not to be taken out of a present conversation and into gossip!

8.

"Walk a Mile...!"

That Judgment Trap!

We've heard this before: "You can't really understand what another person is going through (or has gone through) until you walk a mile in their shoes."

Another way to express this observation on Life could be:

No one can truly understand what another person thinks or feels or what drives their actions or re-actions, because no one can ever really *be* in another's head, heart, and life experiences.

We Can't *Be* the Other Person!

No matter how close we think we are to another person – even to a family member or other loved one – we really can't exactly experience what they experience. We might *approach* truly understanding someone if he or she chooses to share deep thoughts or feelings with us or to open up about Life experiences from their past – how they felt about them then, how they view them now. But even then we can't *actually know or feel as the other person does.* We can listen with loving compassion, we can hold the shared confidences in sacred privacy – but we can't really *be them!*

And besides the fact that judging others is unhealthy for us and for our relationships, it's just plain ol' *exhausting* to play *judge and jury* with one's friends and family members!

For many of us, it's easy to take this judging habit a step further and also fall into the ridiculousness of passing judgment on someone we merely view from a distance or meet casually. We decide with a glance if her or his looks meet our expectations of *acceptable* or maybe whether the way she or he acts is *goofy* and *un*acceptable in our world.

Yikes!

That's all heavy stuff: to think or presume that we could actually know anything about what's going on in another person's heart or mind or how their life is playing out day by day.

Judging is an exhausting responsibility to take on – a big burden to *decide* to carry!

That Vicious Thread

When we make these snap judgments and unkind presumptions about another person and whatever ways we find him or her *weird* or *unacceptable* to us, all too often we decide to share our opinions with others. We compound our unkindness with gossip! Our juicy news or cutting opinions can then wind out in a vicious thread of gossip, going from mouth to mouth to mouth…hurting, maiming and defaming as it moves along.

This can never end well.

Eventually, our lame, meaningless, small-minded opinions can result in a lot of people feeling bad, embarrassed, angry and ashamed. There's nothing good going on there!

Judging is such a ready *trap of unkindness!*

But, this is not what we want! This is not the way we want to behave. This is not the mindset we desire to entertain. So, what's the answer? How do we make simple, daily choices in our observations of other people, which reflect our desires to be kind in our thought and in our word? How do we avoid the ugly habit of judging others?

We Choose to Mind Our Own Business!

When we mess up and find ourselves making those unkind snap judgments, we can at least choose *not to speak* what we are thinking! That would be our first step.

Better yet: If we find ourselves entertaining unkind, judgmental unspoken observations regarding family, friends or strangers, we can choose — in the very moment — to turn our private thoughts about others to kindness and generosity!

We can choose to mind *our own* business!

With our thoughts coming from this attitude, we will then ultimately *speak only kindness!*

There's a Difference!

Let's be clear: It's one thing to judge others just to mentally meddle in their lives or to be an unkind gossip; it's another to use our casual, human observations of others' activities and choices to better *discern* (judge) how to improve our own actions, our own life.

Our basic assessment of anyone's actions, *especially our own,* should be: do they measure up to what we hold to be kind, honest and true?

And, although our personal determinations about how to conduct ourselves are usually kept private, sometimes there's a reason for our opinions about others' behavior to become public, as when someone we observe is bullying or harassing another. Then, we must make our judgment call and speak up! (See our chapter 10, *When the Wall Is So Huge. A Special Note on Bullying*)

So, there are times when judgment — weighing, measuring and discerning — is a good thing: when it prompts us to behave better ourselves, or when it moves us to speak up in the face of wrongdoing.

Bringing It All Together — The Bottom Line!

There will likely be a few occasions when we realize we've "done it again" — we've slipped over into that trap of unkindly judging others! Perhaps we've even (yikes!) taken our moment of needless, unkind judgment a step further into the ugliness of gossip. However, there is hope for us to break this tendency and we can begin immediately to get it right!

- We can remember that since we can't ever exactly walk in another person's footsteps or enter another's head or heart, we have no true thorough reality about what someone else is feeling, what they experience or why they act as they do.

- We can *stop* our rush-to-judgment right in the moment — we can choose *compassion!*

- We can decide immediately to stop our inappropriate judging and simply mind our own business!

- We can try always to think, act and speak from kindness — and with that, the habit of judging others can be just about done away with.

We can simply choose The Etiquette of Kindness in action: treating others as we believe we'd want to be treated in a similar situation.

Discussion Opportunities:

Within your family or classroom or among interested friends and without disclosing confidences or sharing names, discuss times when you've realized that you slipped over into the trap of judgment. Talk about how you felt once you became aware of what you were doing. How did you deal with it, especially if it became an ugly instance of gossip and hurt feelings? Discuss instances when you have become aware of what you were doing and been proud to have stopped yourself in mid-judgment!

Consider and discuss the difference between the unkind judging of others — and judging as a tool for discernment of what to do and not to do; of determining what choices to make in Life. While still maintaining the respectful stance of not disclosing others' private info, give instances in your life when you have used your power of discernment to make an important positive judgment call.

9.

Of Sticks and Stones

And Words That Hurt — or Help!

Basic to learning and living our Etiquette of Kindness is thinking, acting — and speaking! — in ways that include others and include them *kindly!*

All of us have been surprised at some time or another by another person's unkind or unthinking words.

And, from time to time, we realize that *we've* used words that took another person by surprise and caused discomfort, misunderstanding or outright hurt or anger. We may have even surprised *ourselves* by the words we heard coming out of our mouth — even as soon as we said them! (Another *yikes* moment!)

There's that old rhyme: "Sticks and stones may break my bones, but names can never hurt me." Ah, but we know that is not true! Words — ours and those of others — are powerful! They *can* hurt!

When we choose our words thoughtlessly or when we put them together without care, then hurting, wounding or angering can be the result – and sometimes with long-lasting impact! It happens.

However, with our Etiquette of Kindness we can learn the many skillful ways to better use the power of our words.

A Matter of Awareness, Desire, Deciding, Practice!

It's not difficult to use our words kindly, to use them in ways to offer empowerment, encouragement and respectful recognition of others.

- It takes *awareness* of the great impact that words can have to either help – or hurt – and awareness that *sometimes the impact of our word (good or bad) is felt for a lifetime!*

- It takes the *desire* to have our words only leave another person with good feelings about herself or himself.

- It takes *deciding* to choose our words so that we can express what we want and be heard as we hope.

- It takes a bit of *practice*, too, so we can confidently and smoothly make word choices.

Let's get on with determining positive ways we might use our powerful words.

Oops! Watch those Words!

Crystal really likes the way *Lila's* new outfit looks on her, so she decides to say something:

"Hey, Lila! That sure doesn't make you look fat – and it's a cool color!"

Now, this probably could have been worse; for instance, if Crystal had added either *so* or *very* in front of the word *fat*. Since she knows her friend is self-conscious about her weight, Crystal probably thought she was really doing a nice thing by complimenting her on her color choice and by mentioning that she thought her friend didn't *look fat* in her new clothes.

But, because of the words she chose and the way she put them together, undoubtedly, her friend didn't feel very good about this *sorta compliment!*

We *Can* Choose Better Ways!

Crystal could have chosen many versions of a better way to say that she liked Lila's new outfit and how she looked that day.

One possibility might have been:

"Hey, Lila!" That's a great looking outfit! It looks good on you; you sure picked a cool color – really nice!"

Or another possibility – which goes further in supporting and encouraging her friend, as the compliment also mentions a characteristic talent of Lila's:

"Lila, that's a great outfit on you! It's very flattering! You sure know how to pick colors; it must be your art talent coming through. Good going!"

Or, perhaps:

"Oh, Lila, that long vest is great-looking! Terrific 'look' on you and the suede is cool! I'd love to know where you found that!"

Or, maybe this:

"Lila! How do you do it? You find such great-looking clothes and you know how to put stuff together. That looks terrific on you!"

When Crystal chose her words with greater thoughtfulness, she was able to convey her admiration and liking for her friend – and Lila undoubtedly heard this and felt good.

There are many ways to not be hurtful as we make an observation. It just takes awareness, a desire to be kind – and practice!

"You always...!" or "You never...!"
Watch out for those *You Darts!*

There are a couple of phrases which, used incorrectly and used to open a conversation, can be *deadly* to another person's hearing us! Those would be the phrases, "You always..." or the words, "You never...!" as in:

> "You always do that...!"
> "You always forget...!"
> "You always say that...!"
> "You never remember...!"
> "You never (insert whatever *failure* we're accusing the other person of committing!)...!"

We want to be careful of these negative *you* phrases – the *you darts!*

We can't be heard when we are righteously throwing *you darts* at another person – they are too busy defending themselves and trying to dodge the anger and frustration we are aiming at them!

We know ourselves, when someone starts off with "You always..." or "You never..." or any of the other complaining, whining – maybe even angry – *you negatives,* we right away put up our guard to protect ourselves from whatever is coming next! If the other person has a valuable observation, we will likely miss it, as we are understandably busy defending ourselves from their negative, attacking language.

We Haven't the Right!

We don't want to be put on the defensive – and other people don't enjoy it either!

There's no justification for, and it's not correct or kind to brand another person as a terribly lacking, *weird* or *bad* person who *always* does some negative or awful-in-our-opinion thing! Besides the complete wrongness of it, we just don't know how our *labeling* someone might hit that other person emotionally. We have no idea if the other person is feeling very vulnerable and down when we happen to throw our maiming *you dart* of accusation and labeling in their direction.

We have no right to attach negative labels to another human being!

Branding someone as *always mean/stupid/lazy/boring/selfish*...is not helpful! This approach will not *make* someone do differently. Labeling cruelly won't encourage her to become what we might consider *a better quality person*. Harping and yelling won't enable him to *hear* us and become an *empathetic listener* – quite the contrary, in fact!

What to Do Then?

It is tempting to just want to have a small fit when we repeatedly feel frustrated or disappointed by our expectations of someone else. That's not a healthy or productive place to be in our thoughts or actions, but that reaction is common and understandable since it seems so *natural* to automatically respond dramatically and defensively when we believe we are *right!*

However, if we want to have a relationship with that other person, we'll want to select an approach that's different from just letting off steam all over her or him. If there's a chance for them to hear us, to consider whatever constructive, valid needs and desires we might have and to work with us to solutions, then we'll try speaking in a way more likely to give us our desired outcome.

So, what *do* we do if we want someone to hear us or our desire for them to do differently where we are concerned? We steer clear of starting off accusingly with *you darts,* as in "You always...", "You never...", "You don't..." or "You aren't...!"

We pick our words that simply state what we'd like; we don't accuse.

Fortunately, there are some easy, kindly and helpful alternatives to opening comments with negative phrases that start off "You...!"

"I feel..." "I'd appreciate..." "It would help me..."

When we want someone to hear what we have to say, we concentrate on:

* how we feel about their actions,

- the actions themselves,

- what we are asking of the person – how we would appreciate being treated.

Transforming "You always…" and "You never…"!

Let's take some of the "You always…" "You never…" opening phrase examples we had earlier and turn them into words that make us better understood and are more likely to get us the results we'd like.

For instance, if someone were repeatedly borrowing our clothes without asking, instead of trying to affect the change we want by angrily accusing "You *always*…!" we might consider clearly stating our feelings, needs and wishes like this:

"I am *feeling* really frustrated and disappointed! When nothing changes about my clothes being used without my being asked, I feel disrespected and angry! I don't want to feel like that and *I need help* with the situation! When something's taken without asking me, then even if I was inclined to loan some of my clothes, I'd just say 'No!' because I'm so upset and frustrated about being ignored and disrespected. *I'd really appreciate* my request being heard: please always ask me to borrow my things; I can see myself sharing sometimes – if I'm just asked!"

Notice that in the example above:

- we explained how we were feeling

- we stated the problem as we saw it

- we asked for the other person's help

- we were careful to take all opportunities and excuses to use "you…" out of our entire explanation about our frustration and what we wanted to happen.

These general points of positive action can be applied to any situation!

It's Kinder to Be Clear!

Stating clearly what we feel and need and carefully avoiding those accusatory *you darts* in what we are trying to express helps to defuse a possibly angry, embarrassed, righteous response. It's becomes more likely that the other person can hear us. He or she has a chance to realize that what we are asking is what we'd request or require of anyone else with whom we are involved – basic respect and consideration!

Taking this approach goes a long way in building mutual respect, understanding, appreciation – and kindness in actions!

In this setting of clarity and courtesy, solutions are more likely to be found and no one *loses face;* it's win-win, all 'round!

Redeeming the Forgetful or Careless!

Here's a friendship-affirming example for the situation of "You never remember..." We replace those accusatory words with ones more helpful to our friendship:

"Oh, Chris! I feel so disappointed that we missed each other! I really enjoy our times together and don't want to miss out or feel frustrated or unappreciated as I do when plans seem to be forgotten. Perhaps we can help each other to remember? What if we call each other on the day of whatever we are doing? I know we're both busy; maybe that would help us both to remember and to show each other the courtesy we intend!"

In the above example of a helpful statement regarding our plans being forgotten, we:

- start by saying how much we enjoy doing things together;

- take pains to *explain* our feelings;

- don't throw *blame darts* at "you";

- clearly and simply, in a few words, express our frustration, disappointment and hurt feelings – and then move on;

- ask for help in avoiding such disappointments happening in the future – even coming up with an idea of mutual reminding;

- give our friend credit for, along with us, caring about courtesy – and finding ways to make it happen!

"You *always* are so... (cool/wonderful/talented/capable...)!"

As with many things, there is an exception to *never;* and wouldn't you know it – there are exceptions to *never* using that "you always..." phrase. That would be when we want to clearly and emphatically compliment someone on some good thing that they do a lot – when we want to give them a compliment – a "you always..." praise!

This positive use of *you always* we might use in instances such as:

> "Oh, Eric, *you always* know what to say!"

> "*You always* find ways to make me feel better, Crystal, thanks!"

> "Sean, *you always* make nice contributions to our classroom discussion!"

> "*You always* think of cool things for us to do, Sandi, and they turn out great!"

> "*You always* are so kind to my little brother, Mary; I know it means a lot to him!"

When we say such clear, affirming statements, we can rest assured that the other person hears them loudly and clearly! This is a case where "You always..." is mighty welcome.

A Bit of Praise Can Go a Long Way!

That positive pronouncement of something very good that the other person does – something we admire and appreciate in our friend or family member – can leave that person with a wonderful sense of how she or he is perceived!

Sometimes, when we tell such sincere observations to another person, it comes as a complete surprise to them! They may never have known that they so positively affected others in such a specifically nice way – if we hadn't kindly told them so.

So, that's our exception to the "you always..." phrase — when it's kindly, thoughtfully and sincerely said as a *label of you-always-praise* for some small or large deed or personal positive trait. That "Way to go!" will be remembered with warmth, encouragement and pride!

Not to Be a "Downer", but...

Each person here, reading this book and talking about and sharing the ideas, is doing so because they care about others as well as themselves!

We all like to feel good and we try to act in kindness and fairness. We know this and concentrate on *the positive*, but we also need to spend a bit of time right here speaking about some tough, not-so-nice situations that we want to avoid whenever possible.

And, if we find ourselves involved in ugly occurrences in *any* role: as an active participant, as a bystander or (let's hope *not*) as an initiator, we can courageously take clear action to help stop and transform that ugliness!

Because we have the heart and desire, because we have and are gaining more of the knowledge and skills of kindness, we can always determine and then decide how to conduct ourselves.

So, let's tackle some of these not so pretty subjects together!

What's in a Name? Plenty!

When we are thinking from *separateness*, our words mirror our narrow, *them-against-us* thoughts, and often we decide to use words unkindly — sometimes nastily and cruelly — to name, label and isolate *those others over there!*

And whether we think it's a big deal or not, race, gender and/or sexuality-bashing names and words are weak at the least — and hateful at their worst!

We've heard them (and hopefully not used them!) and we know what they are: coarse, crude sexually-slamming and gender and race-bashing words sometimes said in so-called *jest*.

But however these words are used, they *always* spring from their original slang intentions to:

> Put-down
> Maim
> Shame
> Incite to rage
> Cause pain
> Separate
> Isolate

Deciding to use these hateful and bullying slang terms to insult or to shame another person or persons is the exact opposite of kindness – and they say: "I really don't care about you! You don't matter!" and even "You are nothing!"

Our Friends are NO Exceptions!

There isn't a thing cool about linking our friends with sexually demeaning or racially hateful terms. Not in casual *fun!* Not for any other reason!

And, just so we don't miss a thing here, so we are totally clear:

- There's nothing *cool* about calling our friends and acquaintances – either in person or on social networking sites – by crude, rude racially and sexually insulting names!

- Also, it simply isn't true that "everybody does it!" Young people and people of any age with good language skills, people who truly care about others and *people who have class,* just don't do this!

Choosing to use slang racial or sexual terms indicates a huge gap in a person's language skills and usually is *filler* for a lack of vocabulary or for weakness in their ability to express themselves.

Also when people choose to pepper their vocabulary with coarse, insulting words, it's often an attempt to cover their insecurity within themselves; they try in this sorry way to *shock* others and to appear *cool.*

Nothing good comes out of using these insulting terms — and they *don't* add to our *cool status*!

Sarcasm Rips!

Sarcasm, that decision to use harsh, bitter words to "slam" and "rip" others, is a really unattractive and unkind habit.

And *rip* is a good description as *sarcasm* comes from Greek word origins, meaning to *rend (tear) flesh!*

When we roll our eyes, sigh perhaps and make comments about others in a really bored, superior manner, that's a form of sarcasm:

"Yea, riiight...!"

"Oh, suuure...!"

"Oh, you are sooo stupid (lame/dumb...)!" (Or whatever choice of insulting opinion or *slam*.)

In instances such as "That's sooo *retarded (gay...)*", both the *target* of one's sarcasm *and whole groups of unnamed* people are included in the hateful attempts at separating, insulting, shaming and condemning others.

So, since ripping and tearing people is not what we really want to do, we will undoubtedly decide to eliminate *sarcasm* from the way we express ourselves!

The BIG Never-Ending List of *Put-Downs!*

Using words that put down another's intelligence, as in:

> "Hey, Stupid!"
> "You're so dumb..."
> "Lame-o..."

"Weirdo…"
"Hey, Freak…"

…is just plain unkind, rude – and wrong!

In all cases, when we decide to ridicule anyone for any reason it *draws a circle of shame* around the other person. It casts him or her *out there* as *other*, isolated and embarrassed in their miserable state of what we have decreed is strange and unacceptable about them.

No one has the right to try to assign another person into *otherness* and *weirdness!*

So, if we decide that someone is unacceptable because, in our opinion and perhaps in the opinion of *our group*, they are:

> too fat, too thin; too poor, too rich; too ugly, too beautiful; too light, too dark; too black, too white; too yellow, too brown; too wild, too dull; too weak, too strong; too old, too young; too religious, too unreligious; too big, too small; too foreign, too normal; too smart, too dumb; too short, too tall; too feminine, too masculine; too sensitive, too unfeeling; too different, too boring…*too…too…too…*

> …it just becomes too, too awful and too, too exhaustingly unkind!

When we want to create it, the list of possible *put-downs* – of excuses for assigning people to *separation*, *otherness* and *unacceptability* – is endless.

Or!

We can embrace others in kindness. Separation then vanishes like magic – and we are US!

That's our *Etiquette of Kindness in action!*

Discussion and Role Playing Opportunities:

With friends, family or fellow students, go back to the section "You always…!" or "You never…!" Watch Out for those *You Darts!*

Talk about times that you have slipped up and used any of those *you never and you always phrases*. (Please use our rule of privacy and courtesy! Don't mention names here, just the instances!)

> Did you realize as you were jabbing at someone with these accusatory *you darts* that you were whining and griping at the person? Did your complaining *you never/you always phrases* work the way you intended? Discuss what happened.

> Speak about what you might have done differently. At any time in communicating with someone, have you had success with being heard when you intentionally, mindfully took a *transforming approach,* eliminating the *you dart phrases?*

Refer again to the section: "You always…!" or "You never…!" Watch Out for those *You Darts!*

> Role play a scenario where one person is aiming complaining, whining, accusatory *you never/you always you darts* at the other.

> Have the other person react as she/he thinks they would if being attacked verbally with such phrases.

> Discuss how this would work out: Would the accusatory phrases make the other person listen? Would this be a happy exchange? How might each person feel toward the other?

> Now, change the nasty *you darts phrasing* as in our section on *Transforming "You always..!" and "You never…!"* Using the tips found there, phrase your statements courteously and wisely using non-attacking words as you each play your characters.

Switch roles and let each person do a version that's awful, then a good, well-conceived, courteous version until everyone who cares to has had a turn!

Consider using some *you always praise* in your revised versions.

Discuss how each of these instances felt as you played both the negative and the positive roles. Compare what happens with people's facial expressions, how they stand and how their voice sounds.

In this chapter, go to the section *What's in a Name? Plenty!* and also take another look at *Our Friends…, also* at *Sarcasm Rips!* and at the heading *The BIG Never-Ending List…!*

Discuss observations you may have of how people on social networking sites speak to each other.

Do any of your friends or acquaintances use what you consider to be crude language or ugly or unkind names or labels for people?

How does this make you feel? Do you ever ask them to stop? If you have, what has been their response?

Have you ever used crude or unkind labels for others? If you have, has anyone called you on it or asked you to not do this?

If there has been embarrassment or anger over inappropriate labels or words, has anyone said they were sorry and changed the way he/she communicated with you and others? If you needed to apologize and to change your communication style, how did this go? Was your apology accepted?

This chapter, *Of Sticks and Stones and Words that Hurt — or Help!* is an important one! It teaches us to be more aware of our communication skills, of how we come across to others in the words we choose and in our efforts to communicate courteously, kindly and respectfully. Enjoy your discussions and your role playing!

10.

When The Wall Is So Huge

A Special Note on Bullying

Throughout *The Etiquette of Kindness*, we discuss ways to improve our own actions and how we relate with one another — staying in the positive as we learn skills in treating others as we would like to be treated.

Along with all of this very good stuff, we also unfortunately need to know about something not at all pleasant: how to act when we are confronted with the direct *opposite* of kindness — bullying!

Always Wrong – Always Ugly – Always Destructive

Bullying – that attempt at casting out, separating, labeling, demeaning, humiliating, shaming and devaluing – is always wrong, always ugly, and its intent is always destructive!

It can develop into something dangerously abusive!

Bullying attempts to build a huge wall of shame and unacceptability around another person or persons; it can make them feel hopeless, desperately cast out, ugly, angry, useless – and very, very frightened, and very, very lonely.

Bullies are not particular about whom they target – whom they try to maim. Their victims may be people they know well. However, very often their targets are strangers or people they barely know: someone just walking on the street, a person on a social networking site, the new neighbors down the block, or some kid at school.

And, bullying affects not just the bullied, but it also impacts witnesses to bullying, bringing confusion, fear, concern, outrage, and perhaps a sense of helplessness in the face of such ugliness and intimidation. Wherever bullying takes place, it brings misery for all, including those who seem to be simply uninvolved observers.

With its serious dangers and diversions, bullying, when it happens in our classrooms and in our schools, sidelines learning! It can take over countless school days as students, teachers, administrators and parents become embroiled in identifying it and in putting an end to bullying's costly and alarming distractions.

In our schools of course, we should be experiencing encouragement, happiness, confidence, courtesy, respect, opportunity, intellectual growth, wise use of dedicated teachers' time and talents and students' shared and individual pride of accomplishment!

At the very least, bullying always detracts from learning; it wastes school time and energy and brings an element of shame, anger, fear and embarrassment.

At its very worst, bullying can bring social wounding and personal devastation, loss of educational opportunities and the *ultimate* unthinkable: *loss of actual lives.*

Bullying is a huge, important subject and one that is treated in-depth by other people in other books and settings such as schools and religious and community groups. (Note for students, parents and other concerned adults: For further information and professional advice, seek out school authorities and/or mental health and community professionals. Much can be found online, along with links to various knowledgeable authorities and their guidelines.)

However, since the bullying problem is such an important (and sometimes surprisingly confusing) aspect of how people act toward each other, we will talk about it together here, at its most basic.

We, as wise and courageous individuals, will affirm ways that can help us to climb over any wall of shame and separation, thereby helping to bring an end to the loneliness and pain that is bullying!

So Then...

As human beings, each of us has the right to *be* who we are: to look, act, speak, think and express ourselves as we may and as we care to do.

We have the right to be where we want or are supposed to be at any given time and place.

We have the right to dress and appear as we like or as we are required to for any given situation.

And Also...

Let's be clear, that we as young people growing and learning, along with our own rights and creative abilities to think and act for ourselves, have a fundamental responsibility to co-operate with the guidelines and rules of our family group, our school and other community settings.

Our Bottom Line...

Always our most basic yardstick for the way we conduct ourselves, is to try to choose our actions from what we know, and are learning, about treating others with the respect and kindness we would like for ourselves!

So, we have a right to have no bully stand between us and our basic rights, between us and what we know to be correct or what our family, school or other community setting requires of us.

When Our Friend Just Needs to *Get a Clue!*

Occasionally, our friend or someone else might say harsh things and use unkind words, perhaps making unfair or mocking observations or otherwise acting out unkindly. This person may be utterly clueless that she or he is off base and venturing into outright bullying territory!

Sometimes simply calling inappropriate, harsh words or actions to her or his attention will readily set the person straight again and easily stop the thought-less unkindness. We might quietly say something like: "Please stop! Your words are not funny. They're really unkind and I'm feeling picked on and uncomfortable!" Or, maybe a simple, dramatic "Hey! Please knock that stuff off!" might be called for to get the attention of our normally good friend who's suddenly and obviously being *a jerk* to us or to another.

In instances such as this, the person we're asking to stop whatever unkind thing they are doing will often be shocked and embarrassed by the realization of how they are sounding or acting and of how it is making us feel. Often, they are grateful for our calling this bad behavior to their attention so it doesn't become a habit – or so that it doesn't grow into outright bullying.

But, if they don't get it, if they ignore our clear requests to "Knock it off!" or if they are so clueless that they amp up their actions or unkind words, then we are confronting a more serious situation, as this person has slipped over into the dark side of outright bullying! In that case, we'll need to consider our next step in handling the situation. Fortunately, there are guidelines to help us through all of this. Let's continue!

It's Understandable...

We know for certain that bullying is ugly and hateful; it takes *real courage* to even look at it squarely sometimes, to name it and then to take action!

When we are experiencing, or are witness to, a bullying situation, we may be confused about *when to tell and when not to tell.* That concern is understandable.

A young person being threatened or abused needs solid adult help with figuring out what to do about a bullying situation.

Even If...

The bullying person may have big, difficult challenges in her or his life: physical disabilities or family problems or perhaps health or mental issues. But, whatever the situation may be, *no reasons* or *excuses* for bullying are our responsibility – and the *bullying actions* are still not okay!

It's also not our responsibility to protect the bully – to *keep quiet* because we may know him or her and we may feel compassion for the challenges of the person who is doing the bullying.

It *is* our responsibility to call attention to the bullying situation so adults can take over and so those bad actions can be addressed.

Sometimes, our speaking up in defense of ourselves or another even ends up helping the bully by responsible adults stepping in. But, whether that good thing happens to improve the bully's situation or not, it's really none of our business – we must just speak up!

Importantly...

We are *not asking* to be bullied just by our very existence – by who we are or by what we say or do!

We are *not responsible* for a bully's bad actions, and we are *never making them* act that way, no matter what they might say or claim about us!

We are *not ratting on* a bully if we try to get help!

We are not *cowardly* or *disloyal* when we tell on a bully, no matter a bully's claims about our being *a snitch*. We owe a bully's *bad actions* no loyalty!

We are *not better off* not telling! As young people, it may seem difficult and even scary to tell on another. We may feel that a bully's threats to us or to another person are so huge and intimidating that we are safer not saying anything about what is happening. Trying to frighten us into not getting help regarding their bullying is one intimidating tactic used all too often by people who would abuse us or push us around.

No Matter *Who...*
No matter who the bully is:

- a friend

- a family member

- a very *popular* person

- an out-of-control adult

Whoever a bully may be, we owe no solidarity or loyalty when we are mistreated, abused, intimidated or harmed.

A bully might call us *disloyal, a snitch* or a *rat* when we dare to get help with stopping the abuse, but it is just another attempt to shame and intimidate us!

And again, our confusion as a young person confronted with a bullying situation and trying to figure out *when to tell and when to not tell*, is totally understandable.

It's pretty simple:

- Bullying by any person or persons is never okay.

- Bullying has no reasons or excuses; it is always wrong and maiming.

- A young person being threatened or abused needs, and has a right to, *solid adult help* with confronting the bad actions of a bully.

If *I* Am the Bully...

If ever we find ourselves, either as an individual or as a part of a group, indulging in bullying for any reason such as:

- how the *target* looks or acts

- how the *target speaks*

- how *weird* or *lacking* we or the bullying group decides the person is

...for whatever the excuse for meanness, shame and belittling, *as soon as we realize what we are doing...WE WILL STOP!*

We will separate ourselves from any bullying group – even if it's considered an *in* group!

We will apologize and also try to influence the group to stop the bullying.

We will seek responsible adult help if the bullying actions do not stop immediately!

What About Stepping Aside/Ignoring?

Sometimes, either as victims or as observers, young people confronted by an ugly, threatening, abusive situation might feel that if they are *just strong*, if they *don't pay any attention* or if they *just step aside*, the attempts at bullying will simply go away.

That may *sometimes* be the case, and if that works to stop the abuse, great.

But unfortunately, all too often, with a bully bent on getting her or his way or with a group of bullies acting out, the attempt at ignoring the situation or stepping aside doesn't work.

A bully, intent on harm, often labels as *weakness* an intended victim's attempts at stepping aside, and adds the target's so-called *cowardice* to the excuses for continuing with the abuse at the time – or repeating it in the future!

Likewise, a bully's conceit is often fueled when he or she sees observers doing nothing to intervene or to get help for the person being bullied. It's the bully's opinion that casual observers are likely either weak, cowardly *nothings*, not worthy of notice other than as *audience* for the bullying, or that by their doing nothing, the onlookers are supportive of the bully's actions.

A bullying situation can get amazingly ugly and outright dangerous fast! Stepping aside often is not adequate to stop a bully's actions and it's not really a young person's responsibility to try to second guess what might work when it comes to defusing a bully's actions.

Therefore, Here's the Bottom Line:
Bullying Is *Always Wrong!*

We owe no loyalty to a bully or to her or his bullying actions – no matter who the bully is and no matter the situation, relationship or excuse!

A bully is anyone who:

- tries to shame us, to interfere with who we are and how, when, where we choose to be, think, speak, look;

- uses meanness, unkindness and/or verbal or physical abuse to threaten or intimidate us or another;

- attempts to keep us from conducting ourselves as we are required by our school, family or community.

Bulling in any scenario is NOT okay! Whether in person, in writing or online in social networks, there is no excuse for bullying; it harms everyone – victims and observers!

Anyone who bullies another is wrong, entirely out-of-line and needs to be stopped short. Bullying is not to be tolerated.

> We have the right – and we are strongly encouraged – to take any bullying situations to a trusted, capable adult to get help with the problem!

No one needs to put up with the poison of being bullied! It's courageous and strong to stand up against bullying!

Let's Recap to Be Certain We Are Clear!
In any case where we are involved in (or observing) the bullying of others:

- If we ever find ourselves starting to belittle, berate, torment, harass or *bully* another person for any reason, we will STOP and *apologize sincerely.*

- If we ever find ourselves part of a group of young people gathered in bullying another young person or persons, using spoken words, written language or physical presence to intimidate, taunt, terrorize or frighten … *we will stop immediately!*

- We will separate ourselves from any bullying group and ask them to stop their cruel actions – *now.*

- If the bullying/tormenting actions don't stop at once, we will not wait; we will get adult help.

- If that adult doesn't provide assistance, we will keep asking until we get the attention of a responsible adult who will address the situation.

In the case of someone bullying us:

- If we are the victim of a bully or of a verbally-tormenting, bullying group, we will ask them to stop.

- We can choose to try to avoid the bully or to just ignore those bullying taunts toward us, understanding that *occasionally* that approach will work to put a quick end to the bully's hurtful indulgence.

- We also realize that many times avoidance or ignoring doesn't work, that it will sometimes prompt a bully to try harder to get the *victim* to *crack,* resulting in an increase, not a halt, to the frightening, threatening actions.

• If we've asked a person to stop the bullying or if we've chosen ignoring or avoiding the bully and they continue with their actions – we will get responsible, supportive adult help.

• In the case of any physical bullying or threats of physical abuse:

> Always, in any situation where there are *threats of or where there is actual physical harm* (hitting, pushing, physical intimidation of any sort) we will *not* try to handle this situation ourselves; we will get adult help!

Our Powerful, Courageous Community of Kindness!

Kindness can be our basis – our *bottom line* of living! Though unkindness and bullying actions may show their ugliness all too often in our world, let us remember that *with practicing kindness ourselves*, we can actually make a positive difference right where we are – and help to wipe out bullying at every level!

When we use the great power of our words kindly; when we think, act and speak from kindness, from *us* instead of *them;* when we choose to act in generosity, consideration and love, one person at a time…and then one more person… and one more, then *together* we will make a huge positive difference in our world!

Gathered in kindness – as a powerful *courageous community of kindness* – we can help to tear down walls of separation.

Joined in kindness, we can see all forms of hatred, incivility and *un*-kindness, including bullying, become very small, relatively infrequent and unusual occurrences!

This is what our *Etiquette of Kindness* is all about – using kindness and consideration to open opportunities of greater happiness for us all! It's no small thing, indeed!

Discussion and Contemplation Opportunities:

With your family, friends or school group, discuss how bullying creates walls of separation and unhappiness.

Talk about your feelings and concerns when confronted by a bullying situation. Share how you've felt on any occasions when you've either been the victim, an observer – or a perpetrator of bullying.

Discuss any feelings or concerns regarding *telling* or *snitching* on a bully. Talk of how deciding to stand up against a bullying instance – how seeking help, if needed – has worked for you and for others involved.

For your consideration and possible discussion, go back into this chapter; take another look at: *When Our Friend Just Needs a Clue; Even If...; What About Stepping Aside/Ignoring; Therefore, Here's the Bottom Line; Let's Recap...* Or, go back to any of the sections in this chapter and discuss the content, your questions, experiences and observations.

Discuss how kindness is our "bottom line" of how we treat each other. What are the ways that our Etiquette of Kindness can help us avoid and possibly transform bullying situations?

Consider how you might more fully, uprightly and respectfully live our Etiquette of Kindness and be a vital part of the powerful, courageous community of kindness!

And finally, here's to you and to all of your efforts to join in creating a world that is free of the hurt and pain of bullying! *Good for you!*

11.

Those Essentials

"Please..." "May I...?" "Thank you...!"
(And Other Important but Simple Ways
We Show We Care!)

Three essential phrases: "Please...", "May I...?" and "Thank you...!" smooth things out for us and for others. They set a cordial, agreeable tone and help bring cooperation!

When we ask or make a statement using these words, it shows that we care about the other person's feelings and needs – and not just about what *we* want at any given time.

It's always good to be courteous and to use these words of graciousness and kindness sincerely.

"Please, may I have that book?" is much preferred over: "Let me have that book!" or "I want that book" or maybe "Give me that book!"

"Let me have it!" or "Give it to me" is just offensive! An insensitive demand such as this puts others on the defensive and makes them less likely to be helpful or cooperative. "May I have it, please?" simply sends an entirely different message of respect, patience and caring about others' sensitivities and desires!

It's ALWAYS Good to Be Grateful!

It is *always* correct, needed and basic to say "thank you!" in the moment of any type of kindness, consideration or generosity – and to mean it! We say "thank you!" when we are given:

- Small gestures of courtesy in any day-to-day setting.

- Gifts of time, thoughtfulness, generosity, sharing – all of which should be acknowledged in the moment.

- Larger gestures of kindness which deserve not only a "Thank you so much!" in the moment, but *also* a more formal "thank you again!" for any physical gift given or for any notable act of kindness, generosity and thoughtfulness.

(For detailed *how-tos* and tips on when, how, why and to whom to say "Thanks so much!" see our chapter 6, *Thank You! Writing Letters and Notes...*)

These words of gracious gratitude are universal in their preference, appreciation and appropriateness; their use has no age or gender limitation! Men and women, children, boys and girls, young people and old should say "thank you" as a part of their daily habits of speaking and responding.

Those Seemingly-Simple Acts of Kindness and Courtesy

Likewise, we should all be aware of and generous in our offering of simple acts of kindness and consideration.

Courtesy and thoughtfulness *always* apply – without gender or age discrimination!

From little kids to young adults to our elders, all women and men and all girls and boys appreciate being offered kindness and courtesy – it makes us feel good!

Often, a simple gesture of courtesy given to us makes us more aware of being courteous ourselves, and we are prompted to pass along an act of thoughtfulness to others. From one thoughtful, courteous person to another, kindness grows!

Daily, we find opportunities to offer kindly acts such as:

* Opening or holding a door for another person.

* Helping someone on/off with his/her coat or jacket.

* Assisting in carrying items or relieving another of a heavy burden.

* Getting up in open seating (waiting area, train or bus) to offer another person our seat.

* Offering a place to sit to a person who may be considerably older, apparently un-firm in stance or heavily burdened – or to someone who is *just another human being* and we are inclined to be generous and helpful.

* Sliding in to allow others to be seated easily in a non-assigned row or, at the very least, rising or adjusting in our seat to ease others in being seated.

* Offering a hand to a person who might need assistance in getting in or out of a car, or maybe in crossing a stream of water.

* Offering another person to step in front of us at the grocery line when we are heavily laden with purchases.

Can You Imagine?
Not Everyone Welcomes What We Think Is Help!

Now, we understand that some people, sometimes, may not welcome our offer of help or assistance. In fact, our perceptions of what is *help* might be very different from another's and our offer might even be considered offensive or insulting! We may find ourselves surprised by an occasional verbal reprimand for our having offered aid.

In all cases, we are courteous ourselves in our response! Whether the other person refuses our offer graciously or not, we don't waiver from being respectful. We don't press what we think should be considered *courteous* and accepted by the other person or what we want in a situation. We respect the other person's thoughts, stances and sensitivities – and we graciously go on with whatever we were doing.

In These Instances Only One Thing Is Truly *Correct!*
We understand that if we have unintentionally offended someone with our offer of aid or assistance or with what we thought was a courtesy, neither party is necessarily *wrong*.

Varying traditions and life situations can be involved in another's negative reaction to what we thought was a courteous act on our part.

What will always be *correct,* however, will be for us to keep our speaking and responses courteous and respectful!

Worth Considering!
It just may be that another's unexpected response to our offered help brings us to new awareness of the variety of other people's opinions, perceptions and experiences.

We may be broadened in our thinking of how we interact in our world as we are seeking to be gracious and courteous. We may realize that our well-meant offers can sometimes be perceived very differently.

Not everyone sees things and acts and reacts as we do:

• Not every woman likes having a car door opened for her. Many do, some do not.

• Not every man welcomes offers of help with his jacket. Some would feel this gesture to be courteous and thoughtful.

• Not every man or woman likes to be assisted with a heavy load. Many do, some do not. Some feel that they "want to handle it, thanks."

- Not every elder or person differently-abled likes to be offered our seat on a train or bus. Some object to what they see as being *singled out* as *inferior or weak.*

Again, in every instance of offering help – regardless of how it's received – the important things are that we are as courteous and kind in our intentions and actions as we know how to be and that we keep an open heart and mind to others' ideas and sensitivities!

Doing Our Best Because We Care!

With all of this in mind, we keep our daily interactions with others courteous!

We remember to say "Please…", "May I…", "Thank you…" in the small and in the large happenings in Life. We try to thoughtfully show kindness and consideration in everything we do. We do the best that we can determine – and we go from there, always developing and always grateful for our *Etiquette of Kindness* skills!

Discussion and Practice Opportunities:

In this chapter, go back to our section, *Those Seemingly-Simple Acts of Kindness and Courtesy.* In your family, friend or student group, discuss the various points of possibility mentioned in that section. Relate instances in your own life that you remember – situations where you showed courtesy and thoughtfulness to someone and it was clear that he or she really appreciated your actions. Likewise, relate how the thoughtful actions of a stranger, a friend, a relative – young or old – made an impression on you. Share how you feel about these and similar small or large courtesies and acts of kindness.

Re-read the sections, *Can You Imagine? Not Everyone Welcomes What We Think Is Help!* and *Worth Considering.* Discuss instances where your "help" wasn't seen as such – where it was not received at all as you imagined it would be! Talk about differences in expectations of courtesy, as perhaps you've experienced in different age or gender groups or in various cultures. Talk about the concept that, in differences of experience or of expectations among people and cultures, no one is "right" or "wrong." What do you believe is *always* correct, however?

Go over the basic courteous expressions and phrases we want to use in our daily lives; decide to become better-and-better at remembering to use these thoughtful communications tools! Perhaps pick a week to be very aware of *thank you* being used, for instance, by you or by others. Determine that, for this particular week, you will say your thanks more often, observing not only the guides of courtesy, but of thoughtful kindness in generously remembering to speak and show gratitude. When that week is over, continue your practice of expressing "Thank you…" then perhaps add awareness and more thorough use of "Please…" and "May I…"

Oh, your kindness skills know no bounds and you are adding daily!

12.

What About Profanity, Bad Language Or Swear Words

In Everyday Communication?
(Surely I'm allowed when I'm really mad?)

Choosing to use profanity, *swear words*, *bad language*, offensive, insulting or *dirty words* is just that: it's a choice.

That choice always colors how others think of us and whether we can be heard!

Maybe we are upset about something or someone and we figure, "Hey, I'm really mad right now! I should have the right to just say whatever I want to, considering what I've been put through! Everyone has the right to blow off steam with whatever words they want under *these* circumstances!"

Perhaps the people around us, our friends or members of our family, use profanity regularly to express themselves, whether mad or not. That could make it seem like it's surely okay since *everybody does it* — right?

There is so much profanity and raw language in today's music lyrics, on the radio, in the movies and television, on the internet and social networking sites, and since many of the people in those instances are considered *cool* and popular — surely, that means it's fine? Again, another version of *everybody does it!*

Not *Cool* but It Sure Can Bring Attention!

If we make the decision to use profanity or to use offensive, insulting *put-down* or demeaning words, others around us often respond with embarrassment or surprise. There may be a "Hey!" or "Whoa!" or "Hey, man (girl), you're really upset!" response. Maybe someone makes a joke about our choice of words; maybe they laugh (or laugh nervously); or perhaps the conversation gets sort of quiet for a moment.

Sometimes, using this *bad* or harsh language shuts down conversation altogether or at least creates long, embarrassed pauses.

So often, profanity makes the person using it look just foolish or immature. Even an adult *letting off steam* in such a way can sure look immature!

The point is that for everyone using profanity *is* a choice; it's a choice that calls attention to us and to the way we are expressing ourselves — and, it often doesn't bring attention in a good way.

It's just not *cool* or admirable to use offensive, insulting language or crude names to describe or address people. There are alternatives! It's much *cooler* to be resourceful with our words, to have a vocabulary that is extensive enough that we can find interesting, point-making, clear and conversation-encouraging ways to express ourselves!

What About Profanity, Bad Language Or Swear Words

Throwing Pebbles...

Almost always, throwing in an insulting, offensive slang word or some sort of profound swearing is like throwing pebbles at another person – it's confrontational and an attack. It's argumentative, upsetting for a lot of people and takes any conversation up a level in emotion and in reaction.

Quite often, if we are trying to make a point, as in an argument or hot conversation, our point doesn't even get heard if we drown it out by our own limited choice of *hot button*, confrontational, insulting words!

No One Has a Right
To Bring Fear and Upset!

If we are upset about something and not even directing our *venting* to anyone in particular but others are in earshot, this spewing of profanity can be very upsetting for the other persons who are subjected to our ridiculous words. It's disquieting and unsettling and can certainly lessen the respect that others may hold for us.

And being subjected to out-of-control profanity coupled with rage gets the other person's adrenaline racing, so they feel upset, perhaps afraid and like they want to "get outta here!"

No one has a right to bring that confusing ugliness to another person.

> No one has the right to indulge their temper or foul mood so that others – *young or old, human or animal* – are upset or afraid.

But when instead we choose to express ourselves without profanity, without loud and angry words, *things* settle down and can often be resolved. We and our ideas, opinions, concerns and observations can be heard. Issues that come up in life can stay in proportion and be worked out because...

...Hey! *Things Happen!*

Whether a challenge involves another person or is just some sort of irritating thing we need to figure out for ourselves, taking a "things happen" approach to whatever is occurring, rather than blowing up, gives us a clearer head to figure out how to go about solving our situation.

When *stuff* interrupts our day-to-day routines or our pleasant life, we tend to be offended as if we were meant to lead our life without challenges! We all know that Life comes with the easy and the difficult, the fun and the not-so-fun, the sad and the happy...but we tend to forget this.

Of course, though, things *do* happen, and how we handle them says so much about who we are!

We Can Make It a Habit – Either Way!

When presented with challenges, making a choice to use profanity is a lazy habit to cultivate! Choosing to not use profanity and instead choosing to dig deeper for alternative words to express ourselves might seem harder than just letting go and spewing junky language all around!

Well, maybe it does take a little more self-control, a little more brain power and a little more consideration to not use foul words. But, making a better choice in our words is an excellent habit to cultivate! Habitually deciding to *not* use *bad language* while still making one's point is a kindly and considerate social act, a good vocabulary exercise and a way to *expand our brain power – always a good thing!*

Choosing to make a habit of using *civil* words that don't insult, offend or shock is just way *cooler* and shows restraint, self-control and maturity. People (even our friends or peers!) do notice.

Deciding to Use Profanity – As a Part of "Fixing" Situations

Jake is really upset about something that his friend, *Russ,* has done. Jake decides to confront Russ and *let him have it!* He finds him and *gets in his face,* starting off by saying "*You* know what you did...and..." Maybe he calls him offensive names, using a bunch of words that are *hot button* and *foul language* words. Russ becomes angry and says he thinks Jake is "a jerk..." He doesn't seem to hear anything that Jake is trying to tell him, no matter how loudly Jake talks, nor how *colorful* his language becomes! Russ and Jake finally turn away, each stomping off in self-righteous rage.

Now, we may not know precisely just what Jake thinks Russ did to him, but it's for certain that had he not started off explosively confrontational, *in his face* and using "YOU...", it's possible that Jake could have had a much better, more satisfying, outcome.

As it is, Russ didn't hear him at all — or, if he did, he sure wasn't letting on or allowing a discussion. Certainly, he didn't feel like apologizing, even if he agreed that he'd messed up, or if he came to understand that what he had done was uncalled for and not good or *cool.*

Perhaps *Instead:*
We Decide NOT to Use Foul, Offensive Language!
When we make the *conscious decision* to *not* use foul, offensive words, spoken with an angry, belligerent attitude — when we decide to be skillful and fair — we can give everything a chance to quiet down — and to change for the better!

Let's take a look at our little scenario we've been considering where Jake feels that Russ really messed up and was a *crummy* friend in whatever he did to Jake. Jake certainly could have taken a different and better-to-be-heard approach. And, if he had, there's a much more likely chance that both he and Russ would have had a sense of satisfaction, rather than both having gone angrily their own separate ways.

That Finger-Pointing
Accusatory "YOU...!"
Jake could have gotten off to a better beginning with his friend, by using a really tried-and-true approach to opening a difficult subject: he could have taken pains to *not begin his comments with "You...!"*

Starting out with the accusatory "You...!" immediately puts the other person on the defensive! We know how this feels: whether there's actually an accusing finger jabbed in our face or not, that angry "You...!" is inflammatory and we are oh, so ready to angrily counter whatever our *accuser* is going to lay on us!

But, there are alternatives to angry exchanges that get out of hand — when we know how to use skill and courtesy to be heard and understood.

Partnering with Others
In Trust and Respect

As we know in our hearts and experience in our daily lives, we are never in this world alone; we are always interacting with someone, somewhere, somehow. When we approach our relationships, our friendships, with trust and respect and a sense of real partnership, we find many potential problems and upsets replaced by enjoyable opportunities for growth instead!

Taking a partnering, co-operative approach can make us feel happy, satisfied and proud!

Thinking of our friend Jake in our example, here's one of many possibilities for how Jake could have spoken to Russ:

"Hey, Russ, do you have a couple of minutes to talk, man? ...Thanks. I'm confused and feeling pretty frustrated and I'd sure like your help. I'm feeling disappointed (upset/sad/angry...) by your decision to (_____) the other day. I've always known you to be a guy I could count on and a solid friend, so I think I must be missing something here, somewhere. I'm having trouble with understanding why (_____). Am I off base? What was happening, man?"

In our example above, Jake opens his talking with Russ by asking if Russ can give him a few minutes and asks for his friend's help. Jake then begins what he wants to say by telling Russ what he's thinking and feeling, himself; he uses words to describe his own emotions. Then, he gives Russ the benefit of the doubt by allowing that he, Jake, might be missing something or misunderstanding something. He then asks Russ for clarification of the situation, still asking for Russ' help in clearing up the scenario that has Jake puzzled and upset.

Because he cares and has practiced taking an effective, non-argumentative, non-profane approach, he uses skills that are available to us all.

- He *asks* for his friend's *time*.

- He *requests* his *help*.

- He *shares* his own *thoughts and feelings*.

- He *describes* his emotions with specific words: I'm feeling...

- He *honors* his friend by *stating* his respect.

- He *asks* for *clarification.*

- He *partners* with his friend in solving the misunderstanding.

This sort of approach is more about trying to understand and get to the bottom of actions that brought one person discomfort, rather than accusing and *jumping all over* the other person.

Choosing this direction makes it so:

- The *problem* can be identified.

- Each person can be heard.

- A satisfying solution might be found.

- Such a respectful exchange can solidify and enhance friendships.

Now all of that's certainly what we want!

If we change our scenario a bit and suppose that this upset that Jake was feeling came on suddenly, say in the midst of a conversation that he and Russ were having, Jake sure could have put up a hand and said something like:

"Whoa, Russ! Please stop for a second! I'm hearing that you just said...and I'm having real trouble with that, if that's what you meant... "

In both of our *better* examples, *Jake* could be heard by *Russ* because Jake:

- kept his cool;

- didn't attack;

- let his friend know what he was feeling;

- decided against using insulting, offensive, *hot-button* or *foul* words;

- didn't stomp all over his friend verbally and emotionally;

- confronted the situation – courteously and clearly – and didn't let it brew or fester within his heart and mind.

It's Not About Being *Perfect* –
It *Is* About Trying to Choose *Kindness* – Once Again!

Everyone has times when she/he could say things better – or could have left something out, instead of blurting out the unnecessary!

Sometimes, when we are just bombing along, saying *whatever*, we hurt other people's feelings, or say things that sound very different from what we mean; perhaps we even say things that don't *need* to be said! It's good to remember that no one of us is *perfect* and that we all *mess up* from time to time. With that awareness, it's possible to maybe step back from instant anger or offensive response and to cut each other a little (or a lot of) slack!

If we've messed up and started off harshly or insultingly, or if we've chosen foul language to express ourselves, we can just stop. We can say "I'm sorry" and *mean* our apology – and start again, using kind, decent, skillful language.

By trying to act and react in kindness and by choosing our words accordingly, we'll be heard as we want to be heard – with the result that we and everyone can be happier!

Together, we're learning and practicing yet another skill of our *Etiquette of Kindness!*

Consideration and Discussion Opportunities:

Without disclosing names other than your own (we always want to avoid bringing embarrassment or gossip), share with your family, student or friend group instances where someone else has shocked you with his or her blast of profanity. If it's inappropriate in your discussion group, or if it makes you uncomfortable, you don't need to relate the words used, just the emotion and the expression of the bad language. Share how this made you feel: perhaps upset, fearful, outraged, sad, embarrassed, perplexed or helpless.

For some people, swearing or using profanity is something that they just never do; that's terrific and it makes social interactions much less problematic! If that is our habit – being profanity or swearing-free in our speech – we can concentrate on other challenges and attributes that we might have where living with and being around others is concerned.

If, however, swearing is a habit with us, or if it's an occasional indulgence, explosion or cutting loose with inappropriate or profane language, then we can undoubtedly stand some personal reflection – if we care to improve our interactions with others!

Again, without going into detail that would bring embarrassment or cattiness, share any instances in which you let yourself go, language-wise, and "cut loose" with profanity or swear words.

- How did you feel about this at the time?

- How did you feel later, after you had cooled off?

- What did you observe with those around you or with any person who was the target of your anger and lack of self-control in word choices?

- How might you have handled this situation differently?

If profanity use is something you'd like to curtail or lessen in yourself, you might take a moment-by-moment or one-day-at-a-time approach!

- Resolve to change this habit, clearing it out of your speech and eliminating it from your writing – especially in any messaging on social networks where it seems to abound and clutter up the pages!

- See how well you can express yourself without resorting to the shock value of profanity or crude words – there *are* alternatives if one desires to choose differently!

Good luck with clearing up your own unnecessary hot-button, distressing wording in your circles of family, friends and acquaintances! We're all in this together – making more civil, more courteous, kinder and less-abrasive language use the better communication habit. It's a worthwhile undertaking in our Etiquette of Kindness endeavors!

Be proud of your progress! And, if your more gracious speech and writing helps to bring awareness to others, that's also a great side effect! *Go, you!*

13.

Okay, Sometimes It Is About The Right Fork!

A lot of what we'll need to know about: Dining Skills & Table Setting How-To's!

There's no *magic* to make us look good in a social situation or to help us to feel comfortable or to *fit in!*

We can't pull social skills out of a hat at the last moment like some fancy, schmancy rabbit!

It takes a little bit of work and attention to be a competent, confident diner, guest and host.

If we know what to do in particular life and social settings, if we have an idea of *what, when* and *how,* then we can always elect to use those skills. We can be *confident* — and we can be ready-enough for anything.

It becomes simple!

Knowing how to conduct ourselves in something as fundamental to human life and social interaction as eating and dining together is one of our necessary etiquette lessons.

Getting these dining basics down will help us to relax and be comfortable just about anywhere.

Because sometimes it really *is* about knowing the right fork (or spoon, or how to use chopsticks, or when to use *no* eating implements)!

Tea with the Queen!

A young woman I knew was the daughter of especially caring and capable parents. As part of their parenting their children for Life, they taught their daughter and son manners and some fine points about etiquette. Occasionally there was laughter between the kids and good-natured complaining to the parents about the oh-so-proper manners they were learning. Especially, jokes were made regarding *fussy* things like holding one's teacup with the little finger extended *just so!*

But, the wise parents good-naturedly persevered with the etiquette they hoped would become habitual with their kids. They told their son and daughter that "Someday, you may very well be glad you know how to behave in any setting, as you never know what opportunities Life can have in store for you! So *just in case...*"

The children grew into capable, caring adults; the son became a talented, skillful teacher; the daughter worked hard in college and pursued a career in the diplomatic corps of the US Department of State.

Early in her diplomatic career, the daughter was sent to England for her job. She called home shortly after arriving to *thank* her parents for all of their particular, *very proper,* "just in case" etiquette training.

Their daughter told them that one of those *just-in-case* opportunities had indeed come along: she had been invited as a guest for a formal function at Buckingham Palace – to have tea with the Queen! This young woman was happy that she didn't feel unsure of how to behave in such a setting. She reported that she was confident enough in her etiquette skills that she was able to relax, be a graceful guest, do her job as State Department representative and enjoy herself even in such formal surroundings.

Holidays with the President of the US!

Other young family friends, whose parents were involved in Washington, DC diplomatic and political circles, also had occasions to be glad that they knew how to act in formal surroundings. As teenagers they were invited to accompany their parents to White House holiday celebrations. Meeting the President and his family, as well as greeting and interacting with other guests of the First Family was not scary to the teens – they were prepared with etiquette skills!

These young people were confident. They knew that they could do very well in any social setting, even in the White House! They too had sometimes joked about the manners and *proper* etiquette their parents and teachers had insisted that they learn and use; but they had paid attention anyway. They knew that it's always smart to be skillful – including in etiquette!

For most of us, our futures won't hold teas with the Queen or holiday parties with the President. But we can likely expect shared dinners with our friends' parents, important interview meals with a prospective boss, or a meaningful date perhaps involving a nice meal at an upscale restaurant. Wherever we may find ourselves, we can always be self-confident if we are sure of how to conduct ourselves – and what fork to use for what!

It turns out that sometimes it *is* about the right fork, or about how we stir our tea, or a myriad of other etiquette fine points that we may wish we knew.

Cultural Contrasts

As in many things, it's tempting to think that *our* traditions and requirements of dining manners and eating etiquette are the *best* or only *acceptable* ways of eating and dining together.

However, what various people around our world consider *proper, gracious* and *logical* is a study in contrasts of traditions and acceptability. For some, sitting very straight in Western chairs pulled up to an elaborately set table is the proper, traditional way to fully enjoy dining. For others, eating together while sitting on floor cushions and savoring foods served from mats or low tables is the civilized, gracious and logical way to dine.

Slurping of hot soup, noodles and other dishes is considered a logical way to cool them down, as well as a sign of savoring and enjoying foods in Japan and China. But, that action would be considered totally uncouth and rude in an American or Continental dining environment.

In Western/Continental table manners, it's customary to place our napkin in our lap shortly after being seated, but in Hungary, unless it's being used to wipe our mouth or fingers, the napkin is left in place on the table throughout the meal.

It's the dining custom in Brazil to eat most foods using silverware. From snacks to pizzas and sandwiches, all are nearly always eaten with a knife and fork. And, walking around while eating food in public or eating foods in places not designated as restaurants or snack/juice bars, is just *not* done by Brazilians – nor by many other world cultures.

If we are dining in some areas of the world, belching loudly and noticeably is an expected compliment to our host or hostess and a sign of real appreciation of the food we are served! However, belches – soft or loud – are considered rude and embarrassing at most tables in the United States and in Europe. (Let's not try belching loudly at the family dining table, then announcing to horrified Dad or Mom that "Hey, it's okay! It's polite and *required* in *other* cultures! If I were a Bedouin or maybe living in mainland China...")

In the West we eat with our right hand (or our left if we are left-handed), leaving the opposite hand in our lap. But, in quite a few cultures in the world both hands are always left up in view, the forearms (not elbows!) leaning on the table edge when not engaged in eating or drinking. In many cultures of the Middle East, using the left hand to eat is considered *totally unacceptable*; only the right hand is used for eating – ever.

Some cultures always use implements – silverware, or chopsticks – to eat their foods. Other cultures rarely use those, but opt instead to use their fingers, perhaps taking small pieces of flatbread in their right hand to scoop up morsels of foods. And, other peoples in our world savor foods' textures and sensations as they use their fingers exclusively to feed themselves from leaves, gourds or crockery made by hand from local materials.

There is indeed a wide range of eating styles and customs found around the world, all considered to be gracious, logical and correct by the peoples who use them!

Western Perspective

For our purposes, we are taking most of the dining rules and manners from the standpoint of what is usually done in American, Western European and so-called *Continental* dining traditions. This doesn't make these manners *right* and others found around the world *wrong* – the various traditions are just uniquely *different!*

If we have opportunities for traveling or dining in a culture other than a traditional American/Western one, we'll inform ourselves of course! Books and the Internet are ready sources of accurate info. If we use those and plan ahead a bit, we can be assured of knowing what will be expected of us. Then, all we will have to do is take part with graciousness and courtesy tailored for the place and occasion. As a guest or as a traveler, we will then be a welcome addition. Simple!

Dining Together in Our Western Culture
(And Practicing Good Habits When We Eat Alone!)

Dining with others isn't solely about feeding ourselves! It's at least as much about enjoying each other's company, visiting graciously, and savoring foods together.

In dining together, just as in all other aspects of our Etiquette of Kindness, the *bottom line* is to simply try to treat others as we would care to be treated in a similar situation.

If using good table manners is what we *always* do, then gracious, skilful dining etiquette will become second nature to us! With daily practice of good manners we won't find ourselves suddenly surprised, embarrassed and disappointed in our own behavior when we are eating in the presence of others. We will never have to see a look of repulsion, shock and dismay on the faces of our dining partners as we, for instance, try to talk with our mouth crammed full of food! (Yecch!)

We make eating together a nice experience when we practice good eating manners daily.

Here are some basic Western table manners we should always remember – so that dining with us will be a pleasant experience for others!

- We chew with our mouth closed.

- We don't chomp down loudly on chips or other crunchy food.

- We wait to talk until our mouth is clear of food.

- We don't *slurp* our soup or other food as if vacuuming it up.

- We use our utensils (unless we are eating finger foods) to secure bites of food on our plates.

- We use our napkin to wipe our mouth or fingers.

- We don't pick our teeth at the table (or anywhere else other than in private).

- We excuse ourselves from the table to use a handkerchief. (We don't use our napkin as a handkerchief – ever!)

- We try not to make an obvious belch.

Practicing these most basic of Western/Continental good etiquette habits while we are eating alone will make them second nature to us and go a long way in making us pleasant dining partners when we are eating with others.

What! You Expect Me to Remember *All This?*
Our Dining Etiquette *To-Do's* in Likely Order of Need!
Napkin First!

After sitting down, we unfold our napkin and put it in our lap. Unfolding it half-way is usually good; in any case, we don't flap the napkin like shaking out laundry! We'll keep our napkin in our lap, other than to discreetly wipe our mouth or fingers. Even with so-called *finger foods*, we don't lick our fingers; we use our napkin!

Ready, Set – Wait!

Ideally, everyone, including the hostess and/or host, should be seated and ready to eat together; no one starts eating early unless asked to do so by the host or hostess.

A Moment of Gratitude, Please!

For many families and individuals, saying some form of *grace* is a beginning to daily meals. Whether or not an actual grace or blessing is an observance, a moment of gratitude to our cook or hostess or host and to others gathered with us at the table is always in order!

Mindful thanks and appreciation for our food and for the hands that have prepared it always adds a dimension of caring, peace and happiness to the act of eating. This Attitude of Gratitude is good for all and at the very least ensures more pleasant meal beginnings and the possibility of better digestion.

In our Western dining traditions, whether we are gathered around a family table for a meal or dining out with others, it's always appropriate to say, after people are all seated at the table, "Thank you for inviting us to be with you! This is so enjoyable" or perhaps, "Thank you for joining us this evening! Your being in our home is such a pleasure for us!"

Whether from hosts or from guests, appreciation and gratitude are *always* welcome and set the tone for enjoyment and a pleasant meal!

Follow Our Leader!

The Etiquette of Kindness

We begin eating when our host or hostess does. Or, we begin eating if our hostess or host asks us to go ahead before he or she sits down, as might be the case in a casual family setting, where the cook needs to attend to something.

(Note: If we are the cook or host of a meal, it's better to sit down with our guests at first and then excuse ourselves if we need to tend to another food item for a few moments. This allows everyone to begin the meal and creates a more comfortable situation.)

The Outside-In and Top-Down Clues!

Multiples of silverware are seen in a formal setting where there are several — or quite a few — food courses. When we are confronted by more than just the regular place fork, knife and spoon we are used to seeing (maybe there are two/ more forks, two/more spoons and several knives…yikes!), we don't need to panic! With one easy, apparent exception, we can confidently use our outside-in and top-down clues.

> Exception first: for any course, if a food is *served with an accompanying piece of silverware*, we use that for the course served; that piece is taken away along with the dish/plate when that course is completed.

> In general, though: we use the *outside eating implements first* for most of the courses brought to us. From each side of our place setting, we will select the outside, most logical pieces of silverware first. The outside fork (spoon or knife) is used first, then the next one in…and the next for subsequent courses. For instance we'd pick the soup spoon for soup or the salad fork (and salad knife if one is provided) for salad first, then advance inward with each course brought to us.

> The same goes for any silverware we might find up at the top of our place setting: we use these *from the top down*. Unless a piece of silverware is brought to the table along with any final courses of fruit, cheese and/or dessert, we will use our *top-down* clue for those courses. We'll select from the pieces of any silverware (spoon and/or fork) laid horizontally at the top of our place setting; we then select the next closer of these pieces for the next course.

We can also observe what our hostess or host uses for eating the various courses and choose accordingly ourselves.

If we stick to *outside-in* and then to *top-down,* and if we watch our hostess/host for the clues they give by their actions, we'll usually be pretty close to *perfect* — and that's just very much good enough for any situation!

One Time NOT to Share!

Just in case we missed this point earlier, we are repeating it here: we chew food with our mouth closed and we swallow before talking!

This is *so* basic!

We enjoy our food — but we don't *share* the experience with others — it's *yucky* to see half-chewed food as a person talks or chews.

Soup Slurping's Slacking — Usually!

So, our soup course has been served; we know which spoon to use — and we know to quietly eat our soup. As we've mentioned, there certainly are cultural exceptions in the world, but in Western/Continental dining, slurping, smacking and inhaling of one's food is considered rude and crude.

In general, we go with *quieter is more polite* and we try to keep the noises of eating down to a minimum — and *always* chew with our mouth closed!

Body Language!

We are human, of course! Sometimes *things* happen that might not be as smooth and polished as we'd wish. For instance, on occasion, sudden *unavoidable* sneezes, yawns, coughs or belches can occur. In these instances, we cover our mouth with our napkin and we say a quiet "Excuse me," *not* making a *big deal* out of it!

If we can't get any coughs, etc. under control immediately, we say, "Excuse me", *place our napkin neatly to the left of our plate,* turning any food stains to the inside and leave the table for a few minutes. Likewise, remembering that a napkin is *not* a handkerchief, we excuse ourselves and leave the table to take care of a runny nose!

In any case of taking care of needed bodily functions, we will *wash our hands before returning to the table,* where we will we quietly sit down, put our napkin in our lap, resume eating and join in the conversation.

Please! May I? Thank You!

This is easy:

- We ask *please* and *may I* and we ask to have foods passed to us, using those words.

- We say *thank you* when a courtesy is shown to us at the table (or in any situation, of course).

Passing Skills

Normally, the serving dishes are passed from the seated hostess or host and passed from hand to hand counter-clockwise around the table until all diners have served themselves each of the food items.

- A hostess or host will not serve herself/himself from any food *she or he has initiated passing* until it has gone around the table and come back.

- As guests, we help ourselves (using the serving spoon or fork provided – never our own spoon or fork) and then we pass a serving dish or plate of food to the person on our right.

- The person receiving the food takes the offered dish, helps himself/herself and then passes the dish on to the right.

- If the food item has already been around the table and isn't desired by anyone else, then place it is placed in a convenient nearby spot on the table.

Okay, Sometimes It Is About The Right Fork!

Here's what we do if we would like a serving plate/dish passed again:

- If the person nearest the dish we'd like is immediately to our left, to our right or directly across from us, and if our taking an offered serving dish doesn't necessitate reaching across another diner, we can ask for that dish of food to be passed directly to our hand.

  The mashed potatoes that we'd like again are in front of Aunt Suzy; she is sitting directly across from us and one chair to our right. We realize that her passing us the mashed potatoes won't necessitate that our arms extend rudely across anyone else, so we ask her to pass the potatoes, please!

- If a dish of food is farther away, then it's proper to pass counter-clockwise around the table to the person requesting the food.

  Uncle Jack is sitting kitty-corner to us, down at the opposite end of the long table. The gravy bowl is on the table in front of him. We'd surely like more gravy! We ask Uncle Jack to please pass the gravy and he obliges, passing it to his right (counter-clockwise); then other diners help out, passing along the gravy server to their right (without short-stopping it to serve themselves!) until it reaches us.

- When we are finished serving ourselves, we can set the serving dish on the table in any convenient open spot nearby.

Talk Is Good!

Eating together is not just about feeding ourselves! Being a good guest or eating with others includes saying something at the table – joining at least somewhat in creating a pleasant conversation.

- We want to be a part of the conversation at the table – that's the kind and friendly thing to do and it's a part of the sociability of human beings.

- If we are very shy, we still do our best to show interest; we can always make a few comments and ask questions, showing our consideration of others and our pleasure at being at the table in their company.

- Questions are welcome! They are usually easy to think of, demonstrate that we are interested and listening — and they add to keeping the conversation moving along.

- We help keep the conversation positive! Just as is the case with nice music and our body's response to that, pleasant talk helps our digestion! Conversely, unpleasantness or topics sure to be argumentative or disturbing change the chemistry of what's happening in our bodies and makes good digestion more of a challenge.

- Of course, we *always remember* to speak only when our mouth is clear of food!

No Saws at the Table!

For any food that needs cutting we use a knife — we don't *saw* it with the side of our fork or spoon!

Flapping Elbows? No, Please!

When we are eating — and especially when we are using a knife and fork — we want to keep our elbows tucked into our sides and not allow them to stick out. Forgetting this can put our elbow into the ribs of a dining partner next to us, or our arms and theirs can end up bumping. Either discourtesy is a thoughtless "Oops!" that can easily be avoided.

Knife in One Hand, Fork in the Other — but *Which* Hand Is *Correct?*

In the United States, it's common for people (that is, right-handed people!) to eat with their fork in the right hand. Then, when they need to use their knife to cut a food item, they switch the fork into their left hand, turn the fork over, tines down to secure the food to be cut, and cut it with the knife in their right hand. To eat, they put the knife down across the upper edge of their plate (blade in, handle to the right), switch their fork back into their right hand, tines facing upward, and proceed to eat the bite of food. With each need to cut another bite of food, the knife-and-fork-switch is repeated.

Okay, Sometimes It Is About The Right Fork!

This is one common way to hold and use our fork and knife together, but there's another!

Many Europeans and others who adopt the Continental style of dining, including a number of Americans, keep their fork in their left hand and knife in their right all through their meal. They hold their fork in their left hand, with the tines facing down. They use it in that position both to secure food as they cut with their knife in their right hand and to eat – still with the fork in that tines-down position. For folks using their fork and knife in this position, the knife is used not only for cutting, but it also becomes a *helper* utensil, using it to ease food onto the fork. This fork-in-left (tines down) and knife-in-right as cutter/assisting piece, continues for as long as the knife is needed for the food(s) being eaten (often, for the salad course and then through the entire main course). As with American tradition, when the knife is no longer in use, it's put up across the top rim of the plate (blade in, handle to the right), then the fork is transferred to the right hand, tines turned up (or stays in the left, for many left-handed people).

So, both approaches work; both are seen in "polite society" in America, Europe and other places in the world. Neither is right or wrong, but also either may be looked on as *strange* by one culture or the other!

Young people may find that their parents and family have a certain way they consider *best,* or usual, for their daily silverware use and will probably be most comfortable deferring to whichever way is used by their family.

Fingers in Our Food? Probably Not – Unless...!

Generally, we use our fork, knife and spoon to handle our food – unless our hostess or host is treating a particular food as a finger food. Then we *might* take our cue from what they are doing.

However, even something like bone-in roasted chicken can be handled quite well with a knife and fork. Once we get the hang of using a knife and fork to take the meat off the bones, it's easy and isn't as messy as tackling it with our fingers. We use our own good sense, and we may decide to take our cue from our host/hostess. But, using a knife and fork for things like chicken is always acceptable, and, of course, a more formal Western/European/Continental dining setting requires that we use our silverware for eating nearly every food.

So, if our meal is not made up of a sandwich or of *other foods traditionally eaten with the fingers,* we use our silverware — and we keep our fingers out of our food!

Fingers As *Pushers* for Silverware? Oh, No No!

We *never use our fingers to push our food onto our fork or spoon!*

If we are having trouble getting a bite of food onto our fork, for instance, we don't use one of our fingers to assist! We do try using our fork or spoon (whatever we are using to eat the particular food) to gently shove that food bit against another, or we can use our dinner knife to stop the food as we scoop the bite up with our fork. In a casual setting we might use a piece of bread or roll that we are eating to act as a stopper so that the food can be secured by our fork.

But, in any case, we don't want to chase foods around on our plates; ultimately, it's okay to leave a pesky bite or two!

"Clean Your Plate" — Maybe!

We don't need to scrape our plate or bowl clean! It can be fine to leave a few bits or some bites of food on our plates. If we are down to the end of our meal and we have just a little left, we don't *scour* it clean with the fork or spoon, scraping up every last bit!

If we feel that we are eating too much food as a general habit, we might adopt a pattern (at home) of using a smaller, luncheon-sized plate to serve ourselves our meals, enjoying all that we have on this more modest-sized plate. In this way, with taking just one helping and generally not going back for seconds, we should find that we are not over-eating.

In any case, we understand that food is precious; it's taken quite a bit of dedication, effort, water and land to grow it, and more work, energy and thought to provide it and to prepare it. Good food is our source of fuel for healthy bodies. We don't waste it! We enjoy it!

Therefore, we eat our food with appreciation and though we nearly always finish it, from a Western etiquette standpoint it's okay to leave a modest portion of food on our plate. And, if we are full or having trouble with a particular food item, leaving a small amount of our food is not offensive to most hosts and hostesses.

In fact, in some cultures, hosts or hostesses would feel insulted and dismayed if we were to eat every last bite they have carefully served us as their guest! It would indicate to them (and to other diners at their table) that they had not provided graciously with sufficient foods to satisfy our hunger.

Then again, other cultures expect diners to enjoy plenty, eating with gusto and eating it all! In these cultures, dining together is a major social experience and is so much more than just about feeding ourselves; it's about taking a big, luscious bite out of Life! A guest eating just a small amount in this setting might be considered to be ill, unappreciative of the cook's/host's efforts or a very strange, picky eater and fairly antisocial.

So, generally we do the best we can, trying all new foods we are served, being aware and respectful of cultural traditions, leaving little to waste and always expressing appreciation.

Those Pesky – or Fun and Useful! – Chopsticks!

Chopsticks can be fun to use – if we know how! If these are offered, or they are a part of the culture at the table, and if we are able to *really* use them, we can enjoy eating with them.

In the case that we are skillful with chopsticks, we will remember to never stick our chopsticks upright, leaving them standing up in a bowl of rice or other food. (This is seen as thoughtless and deeply rude, as this gesture is only associated with death, funerals and the honoring of loved ones who have died.) We will either place our chopsticks across our bowl or plate or rest them on a chopstick holder, if provided.

If we are eating in a communal dining setting where courses are taken from a common bowl or plate, we turn our chopsticks around and use the fat ends of the chopsticks to serve ourselves, then turn them back to eat.

Of course, with chopsticks, just as with silverware, we never talk and wave our chopsticks in the air – gesturing and jabbing with them to prove a point! Yikes!

If we aren't good at handling chopsticks, we don't want to *fake it* – that doesn't work – we should ask for a fork, please!

Foreign Objects

Any bones or other items that we don't like or which can't or shouldn't be eaten, we take *discreetly* taken out of our mouth with our fingers (not with our fork or spoon as that displays the item for everyone else). The unwanted item is then either placed into our napkin or put onto our plate on the side or under other food on our plate.

Please! We don't say "Eww!" if we find something that shouldn't be in our food – we make nothing of it; we just discreetly remove it.

"You want me to eat *that?*"

Trying many different foods can be a pleasant adventure! But, if we are in a situation where we are offered a food that we know we just can't handle, we either take a very small *taste* portion, or we say "No, thank you." If a food is being passed around the table, we simply pass it along, taking a small portion or none. In any case, we can likely find several foods to partake in at the table, and we are always gracious and thankful!

If we are traveling or joining hosts from a culture different from ours, at home or abroad, it is really smart of us to do a little homework on the foods we can expect to be served. It's easy for us to get a book on the food traditions of the particular culture in question. And whether we will be guests or travelers, the Internet is a terrific resource for investigating cultural food adventures we should anticipate.

One-handed Trick!

In either casual or formal settings in America, we generally keep one hand in our lap while we eat with the other.

Elbows belong off of the table, though we may rest a forearm – preferably, not both in a formal Continental/Western dining setting!

Sleep Later! Enjoy Dining Now!

We sit up straight. We never lie down on an arm at the table or support our head on a hand while *shoveling* food into our mouth!

We raise our fork or spoon to our mouth to eat – instead of bringing our mouth down to our spoon or fork as if we just don't have the energy to feed ourselves.

If we're tired, we find an appropriate time to lie down *after* we leave the table – not at the table!

The *Juggling Act!*

Sometimes, we are confused about what to do with our silverware as we use it to eat the various dishes and courses we find in various meals.

These are the basic things to remember regarding used silverware and what to do with it:

1. <u>Used silverware</u> doesn't belong directly on the table, table cloth or placemat! (We have ways around some awkward instances which we'll share a bit farther on here.)

2. <u>Beverage spoons/stirrers</u> don't stay in the cup or glass, please; we don't leave a spoon in our cup or glass and drink around it – ever!

However! We could find ourselves sorely pressed to follow our first rule if we are drinking a beverage in a really casual environment where there is no plate available. In that case we could find it also difficult to stay with our second rule or suggestion – but, we can.

If there is no saucer or plate provided with a drink we have ordered, for instance, and we have no dinner/lunch/breakfast plate, what to do? Here are some ideas for that sort of situation:

- In this circumstance we might turn our coffee/tea or iced tea spoon over and place it so it doesn't rest directly on the place mat, tablecloth, counter or table top, but so that its bowl is resting upside down on our fork or knife blade (if we have those).

- In a pinch, when we'll be using the spoon or stirrer again and don't want to rest it directly on the table surface, placemat or tablecloth or, we could turn the iced tea or coffee spoon over and put the tip of the bowl on a paper napkin or even on an empty sugar packet (It can work – it's been done!).

Continuing now with more *handy hints* for used silverware placement:

- A <u>dinner or *place knife*</u> that we are using to cut food on our plate is put up to rest its full length across the upper right-hand rim of our plate between uses – with the sharp edge turned in toward our plate. In Western/American table etiquette, we don't put the bottom edge of the handle of the knife (or of any other dining implement we are using) on the table and lean the blade or top end on our plate!

- Our <u>salad fork</u>, if we have one, is kept on our salad plate until we are finished with our salad. If we are served salad in a bowl rather than on a salad plate, we use our salad fork to eat and when we are finished, we rest it ideally on a plate that's been provided under our salad bowl, but otherwise, putting it in the bowl will do.

- A <u>soup spoon</u> also gets the same treatment – it goes in the bowl *only* if there is not a plate given to us under the bowl. A plate under the bowl will always be provided in a formal or even in a casual but more gracious, complete setting.

- <u>Soup spoons and other spoons, knives and forks</u> should stay with the course bowl or plate used. If the course has been served to us in a bowl, such as with soup, salad or fruit, we ideally place our used silverware on a plate provided under the bowl.

- If the situation is quite casual and there is no plate provided under any bowl or cup/glass, we do the best that we can when we are done with using the provided utensil. If necessary, we can place the used silverware on our dinner, breakfast or lunch plate.

Breaking Bread!

When we are served bread or rolls with a meal, we always break them in half – we don't cut before buttering or eating them – and then we eat from one half at a time.

Also, it's not *delicate* or sensitively *fastidious* to break off little bits of bread with our fingers and then proceed to eat them, bit after bit...! That's just silly; we simply eat from the half we've broken off.

Butter Knife Etiquette!

Who would have thought that there could be such intricacies to buttering bread, but it turns out that there's a lot to this simple act!

If one is provided for our personal use at our place setting, this butter knife is set on a smaller side plate (the *bread plate*) to the upper left of our larger dinner or *place plate*. We use the small butter knife for serving ourselves butter from a passed or common butter plate or dish. We put that butter we've taken directly onto the side of our bread plate.

If a butter serving knife is provided on a plate of butter being passed, we serve ourselves using that serving knife to place butter on our butter plate. We then proceed to use our own butter knife to butter our bread item.

We use our butter knife for buttering our bread or roll – but we don't cut our bread or roll with it – ever!

If in a very casual setting where no butter knife is provided and likely no bread plate is provided as well, we serve ourselves with any serving knife that might accompany the passed butter or with our own dinner knife if no other serving piece is provided. We still put the butter onto the side of our dinner/lunch/breakfast plate before we proceed to butter our bread or roll.

Again, in a casual or a formal setting, we never cut our bread or roll; we break it in half to butter it and then to eat!

In any case, we always put the butter we've served ourselves first on our plate. We never take butter directly from a serving plate (with our own butter knife, with a serving knife or with our dinner/place knife) and then directly butter our bread! The butter goes first to our plate and then we butter our bread.

Sometimes butter pats or curls are served and a small fork or tongs accompanies them in the serving bowl or on the serving plate. If that's the case, we use the serving fork/tongs provided to place the butter onto our butter plate and then we use our own butter knife to apply the butter to our bread.

It's Very Clear!

Soup spoons come in various shapes and sizes – who knew!

We use a *normal/regular* spoon that looks a lot like a larger version of a teaspoon to eat chunky soups or stews.

Those nifty-looking oval soup spoons, where the spoon's bowl is wider than it is tall, are used to *tip* clear soups into one's mouth *from the side of the spoon* – we don't try to turn the spoon toward us at a right angle and shove its wide edge into our mouth! Yikes!

With either spoon, we dip our soup spoon into the soup or stew at the front of the bowl, fill the spoon as we take it away from us, then move the spoon to our mouth to eat. The reason for this front to back motion is to be less messy with drips. Going from front to back lets excess liquid more likely fall into the bowl, instead of onto the table edge, down into our lap or dribbling onto our chin! It's just a small suggestion for neatness (and propriety)!

Likewise, when we tip our soup bowl to finish any last spoonfuls, we tip it away from us and use our spoon from front to back as we've described.

Of course, with soup eating, as with eating anything else, we lean over to take our bites!

Darling Little Spoon! *Cute* Little Fork!

Sometimes a spoon smaller than a teaspoon is put at our place setting or served with a dessert or a beverage; this spoon is intended to be used for either a formal dessert or coffee course. It's then placed on the accompanying small plate or saucer when we are finished.

Tiny spoons often accompany small strong cups of coffee – a *demitasse*. We use that spoon to stir in sugar; we place the spoon on the saucer when we are done using it.

In the case of formal dinners, sometimes we will find a small fork or spoon placed horizontally, up at the top of our place setting. If both are there, the spoon will face one direction and the fork the opposite. These will be used to eat a fruit or dessert course if no other eating implement accompanies that course. We pick the top spoon or fork to use with the first of these ending courses served; we then use the remaining spoon or fork for the final course we are served.

It's Necessary to Mention!

Scratching...sniffling...snarfling...*don't* belong at the table!

- For scratching of our head (or of any other body part!), arranging of our clothing, playing with our hair or for any other personal fidgeting, we either don't do it at all, or, in the case of a true *need,* we excuse ourselves and go to the privacy of another room or the bathroom; we don't do any of this at the table!

- Likewise, for extreme clearing of our throats, sniffing, snarfling and all nose blowing, or if we are struck by a sneezing or coughing fit, we leave the table until we've taken care of the matter or until it's over.

- The sound-effects of a person clearing out his or her head or chest just isn't the nicest sound and needs to happen somewhere away from the table!

- Some of these things happen to all of us at one time or another; coughing, sneezing or having a runny nose is a normal part of life. It's simply much nicer — and it's expected — that we leave the table for a few moments rather than subject others to the possibility of icky *blow-back* of a sneeze, cough or nose blowing — or to the unsanitary situation of germs being passed on serving dishes!

- And of course, after we've taken care of personal issues of any sort, we wash our hands with soap and water before returning to the table!

Compliments are GOOD!

If there's something we particularly like at the meal, we compliment the cook and/or our hostess or host by mentioning it. An observation that we think something is attractive or delicious is always appreciated. If, one day, we find ourselves in a large, super-formal, official dining setting, we would make such comments only to our immediate dining partners: "Aren't the flowers and candles lovely!"

Nearly Done with Our Dining Experience!

When we are finished with our food, and if it's been a meal eaten with silverware (instead of a sandwich, for instance), we:

- Place our used silverware across our plate, in the middle of it but with the handle ends on the right-hand rim and at an angle that corresponds approximately to the small and large hands at *3:15* on a clock face.

- Bring any place/dinner knife we've used down from the top rim of the plate; we turn the knife blade so it faces down in the direction of ourselves, not up toward the middle of the table.

- Turn our fork over, tines down, and place it under the knife and if a spoon is involved we do the same with that, turning over the bowl of the spoon to face down toward the plate.

- Place our napkin back on the table, either to the left of our plate, or if our plate is removed, we place it in its spot. We don't need to fold it as it was; we simply lay it neatly at our place, turning stained areas to the inside. This way, our place looks neat, clean and pleasant to the eye as we leave the table.

Grand Finale!

We *always* thank our host and/or hostess. We say something like: "Thank you, so much! I really enjoyed our meal together; it was very good! Thank you for inviting me…" (Or whatever we think is an appropriate "thank you!" in the circumstance.)

Our mom or dad always likes a compliment and thanks, too, so we don't forget our parents! We thank our family member who prepared our meal for making it for us; we say something complimentary about the nice meal we have just enjoyed.

Our Final Request!

As a young person, when we are finished with our meal and we want to be excused, we ask: "May I be excused, please?"

An adult who needs to leave the table early would simply say her or his thanks and perhaps "Excuse me for leaving right now, but…"

Laying It All Out!
We *Always* Pay Attention!

Since we are people who care, we have that attitude when it comes to setting a table and laying out food for ourselves and for others. No matter for what meal, we pay attention to making things work well and to having them look attractive!

It's Not *Right*, but…!

We should point out that in table setting, as with so many things in our world, it's all based on *everyone* being right-handed! We know, of course, that this is not correct — many people are left-handed. But, *silly* or not and *fair* or not, table setting is based on arranging things for the convenience of the right-handed.

It's Even!

When we set a place at a table, we try to keep all the silverware laid out evenly, with the bases of the different pieces aligned with each other across an invisible bottom line. The place plate or the breakfast, lunch/salad or dinner plate, which is in the middle of the individual setting, is set to align approximately with the same bottom line as the silverware.

Whatever we do on one place setting we will repeat around the table, so the table lay-out is balanced and pleasing to the eye.

And, if we are laying out more than one table, we will want to follow this same even pattern of placement at every place setting. Keeping this layout consistency, even if there are several different types of china or glassware used in the room, ensures that our eye sees harmony when it sweeps across the tables. It's a subtle thing, but if we didn't take that careful approach, the difference between haphazard and even placement would show up immediately!

Our carefully-placed settings show we've taken care to prepare our table — and our care says "Welcome! It's a pleasure to have you here!"

Flowers Are Nice!

A small or large bit of Nature or any touch of beauty is always a good thing to bring to the table!

Flowers, either picked from our yard or purchased, can add color and spirit and can be great fun to arrange artfully.

We could also choose a variety of things for the purpose of adding beauty to our table: shells, attractive leaves, candles, a lovely piece of wood from the countryside or seashore, a mirror placed flat on the table, a small collection of pretty bottles, interesting branches...Anything that is pleasing to our eye can be used to create a nice focal point on the table or at a place setting.

Using short *elevations* of our centerpiece can sometimes be nice, varying the height of the different elements that we are using. Whatever we decide upon, we'll want to be certain that the flowers or decorative elements are kept at a height that doesn't interfere with diners' views across and down the table.

We can coordinate our selections to a celebration of a birthday, a season of the year or to a special holiday. All of these occasions can help us to get inspired about how our table will look.

The effort of enhancing our table doesn't need to cost any money, or very little, but it does entail our *investment* of a bit of thought and attention! The extra care and detail of these added touches bring so much to a dining table; they say "I care!" and "Welcome!"

Napkins *Not* Optional!

Using our clothes, or the backs of our hands, as a place to wipe our messy hands and fingers when we are eating, is not cool! Even if we are just taking a sandwich in hand to eat outside, we always have a way to catch crumbs (a napkin or even a basic paper towel) and to wipe our mouth and fingers, so we don't leave food stains and trails as we go out the door.

From formal dining through informal family meals to casual picnics, we always have a napkin. We provide them when we are responsible for the foods of others, and we *always* include them in any table setting.

Napkins can be paper or cloth. Solid colored or patterned, cloth napkins can be found that are easily washed and refolded, not requiring ironing or pampering to look presentable.

If a person cares to, there are dozens of fancy napkin folds that can be easily learned. It can be fun – but it's not necessary to make a fancy fold to have an attractive napkin at a place setting.

When folding a napkin to place simply at the left side of the plate, or to lay flat on the center of a dinner plate, we fold the napkin so that the nicest side is facing out (the side of the cloth that we see should be the *right side* of the fabric). With a napkin folded into a long rectangle and placed either on the left side or on the plate, we keep the rounded fold on the left of the folded napkin; the layered edges of the napkin are facing in to the right, but unseen. From the top, the napkin looks neat and tidy.

And again, balance is important in this aspect of table setting, too. If there's a pattern to the napkin we are using, we make certain that the napkins are all folded with the pattern going the same way. That way, when they are laid at the various place settings, the repetitive end result will be eye-pleasing and balanced!

Ready, Set!
(What goes where; from basic simple settings to the fairly formal stuff!)

Though on occasion we might use something as simple as a plate with a sandwich on it (and a *napkin alongside* please), often we need a bit more to set our places at a table. Let's take a look at some possibilities, going from really basic and casual table setting first… right on through quite a formal setting.

Quite Casual

Sometimes, whether it's a meal of breakfast, lunch or dinner, we have just a few foods and all food items fit nicely on one dinner or luncheon-sized (smaller than dinner) plate. In this case, we might have a simple glass of water or juice or other beverage along with our meal.

For our very informal family breakfast, lunch or dinner, we might set our table as in this illustration, with no side or salad plate or soup bowl.

If we wanted a pasta/soup bowl to hold our simple meal, it could replace the lunch or dinner plate in the middle of the place setting. If we wanted to take our place setting up a notch in niceness, rather than just placing the large soup/pasta bowl there by itself, we could slip a plate under the bowl for a convenient and more attractive place to put our used utensils, other than merely in the bowl itself.

Quite Casual Place Setting (for a breakfast, lunch or dinner)

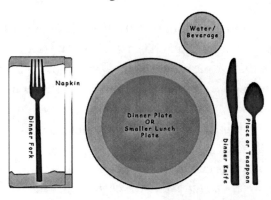

Okay, Sometimes It Is About The Right Fork!

(Note that the bottoms of the plate and the silverware all are in approximately the same horizontal line. The napkin has a pleasing relationship to this line, as well; it could also be put on the plate, at the center, if desired, with the fork on its own in its place on the left.)

If we are setting a place for a very simple breakfast, say of cereal or yogurt with fruit, we might just lay out a spoon, a glass *and a napkin*, with the bowl of cereal in the middle, either with a small plate under the bowl or with no plate at all, just the bowl. If we are having toast along with our cereal though, we will want someplace to put it — other than laying it on the table/place mat or table cloth! In that case, a plate either under our cereal bowl or out to the upper left hand side, above our napkin, would work for our needs.

If a mug or cup and saucer are needed for coffee, tea or perhaps hot chocolate, then the mug or cup and saucer would be placed to the right of and slightly below the water or beverage glass.

Super-simple Breakfast Setting

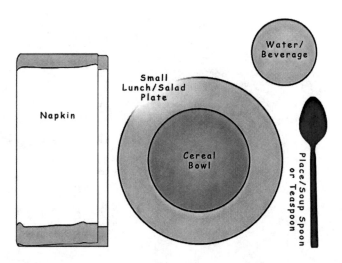

Please note, again: even in this super-simple place setting, the various pieces line up nicely with each other; they are placed generally in the traditional spots they'd be found in a more elaborate setting. Formal or casual, our place settings always look appealing!

Taking It up a Notch or Two!
A Nice Setting for Family or Guests

When we are responsible for setting the table for our family or for a nice meal shared with guests, perhaps we'll want everything to be set so that the effect from the first view of the table is one of pleasure and attractiveness – and of *welcome!*

With a casual family or company meal, we'll consider something for a centerpiece, even if it's quite simple. Sometimes, in the case of a long table, we might want to place several attractive groupings down the center. We might want to include candles as well.

We'll of course pay attention to all that we've learned regarding evenness and repetition at each place setting! We'll make certain that everything we place is clean and shiny and that nothing is missing for the foods that we know will be served.

Fairly Casual Place Setting

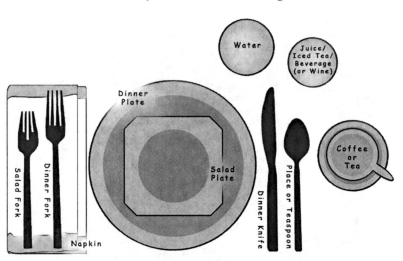

Note: In a very casual setting, instead of placing a salad plate on the dinner/ place plate, a not-too-large salad plate could go up and to the left side, just above the forks and napkin placement. In that case it would be used for a salad or other food item served as an accompaniment *with* the meal, rather than served before. For casual purposes, with no bread plate provided, this salad plate could be used to hold bread or a roll on the side rim, as well. (If a salad bowl were used instead of a plate, of course, it would not serve as double-duty to hold any bread or roll!)

For Our Special, Celebratory Meals!
Bringing out the Best China and Silverware

There are times in Life when only our best will do: birthday or anniversary celebrations, special holidays or congratulatory meals to say "Well done!" It's then that we can polish up the best that we might have in the way of dishes, glasses and silverware.

Even if our *best* is the same tableware as our everyday, we can put extra touches on everything and include just a few more pieces to meet the needs of a more elaborate meal.

This can all be fun and exciting! We'll want to include a centerpiece, of course (or several down the middle of our table, or even small ones at each place), and candles if we have them.

The place setting we show below is quite formal. I would call it *family formal* or a type of *restaurant formal* we might find while dining out.

It doesn't include some elements of a truly formal affair: the silver placed in the top middle for final fruit, cheese and dessert courses; specific fish and/or poultry forks and knives; a special salad knife; more (there could be several more!) wine glasses for the various types of wines served with courses in a very formal meal.

We also don't show a coffee/tea cup in our drawing here, but if that would be desired as a beverage, a cup and saucer would be placed out to the right side, just off of the spoons. We don't show that here, because in a more formal dining experience, usually coffee or tea is brought after the meal and is either placed over to the right side, as mentioned, to be enjoyed along with any dessert, or it is placed in the middle of the diner's place setting all on its own. In that instance, individual cream and sugar (and perhaps lemon, for tea) would also be brought to the diner at the same time.

Fairly Formal Place Setting

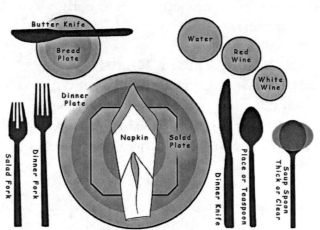

Serving, Passing, Clearing

On occasion, we may need to know the proper ways of serving a table. This could be when we are hosting or helping to host a large sit-down meal for our family or for a civic or school group, for instance. It could also be a duty at a summer camp or for a weekend, part time or full time job eventually.

Whatever the reasons or needs, these skills of serving, passing and clearing graciously are important to know since we are all social beings and since we all want to know how to be skillful in everything that comes our way!

We should point out that serving, passing and clearing are also based on *every-one* – diners, hosts, hostesses and servers alike – being right-handed, which we know of course, is not correct, but it's how these procedures are all set up, anyway! It's yet another case where we need to learn skills, be gracious – and go with the flow!

So, with that knowledge, let's proceed with some handy bottom-line basics to make these things pretty easy!

1. We *never* reach across any person to serve or to clear!

    a.   We do our very best in all circumstances to fulfill this rule.
    b.   Our guests' comfort and ease is uppermost – not our own.

2. We always graciously observe what our dining guests are doing and how far along they are in their course or meal. We never rush them to serve or to clear nor make it appear that one person is slow and should hurry up!

3. With the above in mind, unless we are told to do differently either by our guests or by the person in charge of the dining situation, we don't clear plates until everyone is through with the course or the meal.

4. When placing any plate or course that goes in the middle of the diner's place setting, directly in front of them, we LOWER from the LEFT (side of the seated diner) and we RAISE from the RIGHT (side of the diner). This *LOWER from the LEFT, RAISE from the RIGHT* is a handy reminder for how to place/serve (lower) and remove/clear (raise) a plate or bowl in front of any seated diner.

5. When serving, we always *serve (lower) from the diner's left* and graciously put the plate down in front of them. If they are talking or if they have an arm in the way or if they are taking a drink, we wait an appropriate moment, smile and quietly say "Excuse me" or "May I...?" and courteously place the plate.

   We follow this practice while serving *each* diner.

6. When clearing, we always go to the *right-hand side of each* diner! We don't clear (*raise*) one plate correctly on one diner's right side – and then turn to the next diner on *our* right to raise/clear their plate from their left side! We are not lazy or discourteous! We step around to each diner's right-hand side to clear from their right!

   a. We may quietly take the plate if the diner has given us their *finished* signal of silverware placement on their plate or have asked for the plate to be removed.

   b. We may also ask "May I...?" before taking the diner's plate if no such formal and certain signals have been given. (In this case, we observe the meal progression and the diner for indications that he or she may likely be finished with that course or with their meal.)

c. Remember: we don't "pick at" the table, anxiously watching to see if someone is finished with a course or their meal; we don't keep popping back to the table, clearing here…clearing there! Unless we are asked to do differently, we wait until all diners are finished with a particular course or with their meal, then we begin to quietly clear from all diners.

d. We stack only a plate or two, take them away and then return again. In proper dining, we would never use the table to create a "convenient" stack of dishes there in front of the diners, and then carry it all away for the dishwasher. We remember to *clear from the right-hand side of every diner!* (We don't use our position between diners to clear first from one, then pivot and clear from the other!)

7. If we are *serving anything that goes specifically on the right side* of a seated diner's place setting (a drink of any sort or if giving the person a piece of silverware), we will step to their right side and place the item. Again, if there is anything going on, such as a conversation that crosses the path of our serving needs, or if the person is engaged in drinking at the time, we wait a moment for our presence to be (even subtly) recognized, perhaps say "Excuse me, please" and graciously place the item.

8. If we are *serving anything that goes to the diner's left side,* such as a side salad or bread/roll on a bread plate, or if we are offering them a bread item or butter perhaps, we will step to their left side and ask if they would care for whatever we are offering; if already expected, we will quietly place the item in the appropriate left-hand spot. Of course, if we are interrupting anything, we will wait patiently a moment, say "Excuse me, please" or, "May I serve you /Would you care for …?"

9. Of course, if for some necessity we are clearing an item from the left side of their place setting, we will ask first or say "Excuse me" before taking the item.

10. And, just to restate and to end with where we began: we *never reach across a diner to serve or to clear!*

Whew! That's all a lot to know! But, it's mostly the logic of gracious, kind living and dining with each other – simple!

So Sometimes It Really *Is* About the Right Fork *and* About Creating Dining Adventures Together!

We've come a long way since the beginning of our chapter here on eating, dining and on being a gracious host and a courteous, knowledgeable guest. We've applied ourselves and given a good amount of attention to knowing better how to feel comfortable and confident in many dining and social situations. We know quite a bit more than when we started this section but, there's a whole lot more to know and to experience in the world-wide subject of eating and dining together.

Dining can be a real adventure! There are so many different foods enjoyed in various places in our world. Often, due to today's ease of travel and the development of the Internet, both people and native foods travel a good distance. Either literally or virtually, traditions, recipes, food items and the people who love food and dining move around our earth, impacting and enhancing cultures as they go! It can make for some exciting eating adventures as we find new discoveries for our taste buds!

So, the more we reach out and explore, the more we meet new, interesting people and also gain opportunities to broaden our experiences with new foods and dining traditions, some of which may seem very unusual, indeed!

We find that there are many ways of doing things *correctly* and that different climates, geography and ancient traditions influence the things we eat and how we eat them. If we keep our minds and hearts open to adventure, then we'll be ready to experience from a new perspective what we once might have thought was *unusual*, *strange* or *incorrect*. We can come to see as okay, practical or enjoyable things such as: using our fork in a manner we might consider to be *upside down*; eating salad *after* a meal instead of before (or vice versa); using chop sticks to eat and to cook; eating flowers, seaweeds or insects (yes, they are staples of a number of cultures!); using small bowls of scented water to cleanse our fingers between courses; accenting our foods with pungent spices strange and maybe fiery to our taste.

And all along the way, because we are caring, kindly, gracious people, we take the time to teach ourselves skills and courtesies — including even something as basic as which fork to use when.

We've found that sometimes it really *is* about knowing the right fork!

Since we've broadened our social knowledge, we won't have to pull anything out of thin air as if by *magic!* We now are more confident and comfortable. We know how to welcome others gracefully and wholeheartedly and how to help make memorable and pleasant dining experiences.

We are expanding our skills and courtesies — always having fun while we practice The Etiquette of Kindness!

Practice and Discussion Opportunities:

Take any section in our chapter here and discuss what you have experienced when dining at home, out at restaurants or as a guest in someone's home.

- Have several people (or a family or a class) get together and practice table setting. Perhaps practice a casual family dinner setting. Have multiples of all the silverware you would use, placemats to identify the place setting space, napkins, glasses and plates for dinner. Include, if you care to, plates for salad/bread and butter, mugs or cups and saucers and soup bowls. Adjust the silverware you'll use accordingly.

  Break up into groups, pick out your items and lay out your settings from what you've learned here in *Okay, Sometimes It IS About the Right Fork!* Give participants five minutes or so to finish their setting, then gather and "tour" what everyone has done to create a place setting.

- Pick a country or a culture and research its eating and dining traditions; report back to your family or to your class. Be creative! Share a food item (if you care to), an unusual or beautiful eating implement, a photo... If you've been to that country or dined in that culture, share your experiences. Ask for questions – and ask them yourself when it's someone else's turn to share. Enjoy!

14.

"*Ta-Dah!*"

First Impressions
(How we present ourselves)

No matter what sort of personality we have, most of us would desire to make what we might consider to be a *good first impression*.

Like it or not, and whether or not it is fair, kind or generous, those first impressions do make a difference when we meet and greet others. Let's consider how we might present ourselves as we want to be perceived.

To make certain that we're all on the same page in what we are meaning here, a little clarification is in order: we're not talking about impressing others by how cool or pretty or handsome we are, or how expensive or "in" our clothes or accessories or hair style might be. What we *are* talking about is so much more — and costs next to nothing! We'll see how simple the skill of presenting ourselves well can be; we can confidently create our own satisfying *first impressions!*

It's Really Basic!

Whatever we are doing – getting ready for school, dressing to go to a summer job, going to the store, meeting friends – the first consideration in our presentation is cleanliness. We make certain that our face and body are clean, our teeth are brushed and flossed, our hair is combed and that our clothes are clean and appropriate.

This all may seem really basic, but sometimes we do forget. We think, "Oh, I'm only going out to walk the neighbor's dogs; it doesn't matter how I look." Or, maybe, "It's only my friends; they won't care."

But, it's a fact of social life that, rightly or wrongly, people do notice how others look or present themselves. They do have opinions or make judgments – especially if someone appears sloppy and disheveled, or has bad breath, or should have showered, or is wearing obviously-dirty clothes when not engaged in dirty work like mucking out the horse barn, washing the dog or grubbing in the garden.

No matter what we are doing, we can show our *attitude of caring* with a few simple steps. This will make a huge difference in our days – in how we think of ourselves and in how others perceive us!

Sleep Magic!

Sleep is magical when it comes to making those "Ta-dah!" moments possible. It's very hard to present ourselves well if we are under-rested; it's a struggle to be bright and nice, and we just can't look our best without enough sleep – it's a fact!

Getting enough sleep:

- Makes our lives happier!

- Helps our brain to work its best so we think straight and feel confident!

- Makes it more likely that we are civil and pleasant people!

- Contributes to our presence being enjoyed by others!

Enough sleep provides the opportunity for our body to renew itself, for our skin to glow with good health; it's when we sleep that our body can make the repairs it needs. Sufficient sleep is *magical* in how we look and feel — how we present ourselves!

Get the Good Fuel Our Body Craves — and Thrives On!

It's difficult to present ourselves at our best if we don't take care of eating well! If our body and brain are tired — from a lack of sleep or from being whipped around by a crummy, perhaps sugar-loaded diet — they just can't cooperate with helping to present us as we desire!

But, there's good news! We can make a few simple additions, subtractions or adjustments in our food habits and selections — and we can look and feel ever-so-much better in a short time!

We can kick-start any day into being one where we have a cheerier, friendlier attitude and sharper thinking. Simply remembering to eat a nutritious, *non-sugar-laden* breakfast every morning, such as plain yogurt with fresh fruit or whole grain toast with peanut or other nut butter, can work wonders. Since eating breakfast improves our ability to problem-solve and think clearly, we naturally feel more confident!

Cutting down on any kinds of sodas and fruit drinks and replacing them with water gives our body the fluids it needs. In general, it's also helpful to dilute any 100% fruit juices we do drink with equal parts of water or sparkling water. In this way, our body and brain can gently benefit from the good things in the juice without a sudden jolt of sugar — even natural fruit juice sugars.

And, before we reach for one of the popular so-called "energy drinks", we might want to ask our doctor's advice or at least do some reading on how the human body responds to such heavy caffeine and other stimulant hits. Being always *wired* and always *on* is very wearing to the body — even a young one! And for many people of all ages, high doses of caffeine can cause uncomfortable side effects such as anxiety, aggressive behavior and sleep disorders. At the least, while *super*-buzzed it's difficult to be at our gracious best, interacting with others smoothly, with calm confidence. At the worst, heavy stimulant use can do our body real harm and it's outright dangerous for some people. Please! Check out the info before deciding to gulp down those energy drinks!

To feel and look our best we want to drink a LOT of plain ol' life-giving, cleansing water every day! Also, replacing super-salty or sugary foods and snacks with fruit, nuts or vegetables is a great way to start cleaning up our nutrition act!

And, we should pay special attention to loving and using these health and beauty producers for our meals: daily big helpings of fresh veggies and fruits, any cereals and breads made of whole grains – and enough high quality protein to make our cells happy and our body strong! (Especially consider these protein sources: fish, poultry, eggs, milk, yogurt, nuts and seeds combined with whole grains.)

To help keep our blood sugar level and our energy steady, nutritionists suggest eating three meals daily, each consisting of selections from at least three to four food groups: vegetables, fruits, lean proteins, nuts/seeds, milk or cheese, whole grains. To this we will want to add two or three healthful snacks a day, primarily from the fruit and veggie groups. Apples, grapes, pears, berries (blueberries, raspberries, strawberries…) fresh citrus fruits, carrots, celery, broccoli, jicama, cucumber and sweet pepper slices are all excellent choices. Reserving things like *a few* chips or French fries, so-called *fast foods* and small servings of dessert as an *occasional* (*not* daily!) snack splurge or treat, will help us to have a healthier, trimmer body!

Our skin, eyes, hair, nails, bones and brains will thank us by responding well to our better nutrition, giving us a body thriving with health and good looks and a brain able to think and reason to our true ability!

So, taking a few minutes to honestly ask ourselves whether we are doing the best by our body and mind every day, food wise, is the first step in using nutrition's big role in our feeling and looking tip-top. The next step will be to clean up our nutrition act a bit (or a lot!) – to help us feel and look our vital, attractive best – *"Ta-dah!"*

The Value of Fresh Air, Exercise and Sunshine!

Helping us to feel vital and positive is something right outside our doorway – Nature! Getting outside everyday for at least some period, where we can benefit from natural light on our body and in our eyes, let fresh air fill our lungs and stretch our limbs in movement, tends to make us happier, more alert and healthier in general. And, all of those good things also help us to have more confidence – to feel like we look good and like we are ready to greet our world!

Besides, getting into the outdoors can widen our perspectives – literally – as we look out and around us, taking in what's happening and what delights Nature might have for us!

Since health professionals suggest at least an hour a day of active exercise to help ensure better vitality for most young people, that's an excellent prompt to *turn off the electronics* for awhile and venture *outside – electronics free!*

Whatever your level of health or abilities, *at least get outside every day!* Move! Play! Breathe! Enjoy! See what's out there! Unplug and *listen* to Nature! Take in all the positive things that this wide world has for us! There are so many natural, marvelous elements awaiting us outside – all ready to help us feel like saying "Ta-dah! Here I am world!"

Our *Top Ten* – Plus the Big Two!
So, added to a basis of –

> plenty of sleep, good nutrition, fresh air and movement, here are The Top Ten Basics for good grooming and a confident self-presentation.

For everybody for every day, we:

1. <u>Wash our face</u> when we get up in the morning. (And, if we're feeling really overnight-icky, at this same time we might brush our teeth and maybe swish some mouthwash, too!)

2. <u>Shower or take a bath</u> when we need it! We know when that is, and for most people, that means a bath or shower once a day and after sweating a lot or enjoying really dirty work.

3. <u>Wash our hair</u> often enough to keep it clean and shiny and smelling fine (for some people that's every day).

4. <u>Brush or comb our hair</u> and make it neat in whatever style we like.

5. <u>Keep our clothes clean</u> and ready for whatever activities are coming up for us. We remember that clothes that start off smelling a *little* sweaty will only get more noticeably objectionable as the day wears on!

6. <u>Watch those shoes</u>! Grubby-looking shoes are fine for some things (we don't want to wreck good shoes in mud), but we try to keep our tennies or athletic shoes washed or scrubbed, and scuffs on other shoes buffed or polished out. Though we don't wear many shoes these days that need to be re-heeled, there are exceptions, so we find a shoe repair and take in any that are worn down and look *funky!*

7. <u>Pay some attention to our feet</u>! Keep them clean after activities, scrubbing with a pumice stone or other foot grooming aid as necessary. We keep our toenails trimmed. Athlete's feet, smelly shoes and stinky feet *happen* – to both guys and gals! If we find any of this is becoming a problem, we get right on it and seek advice on what to do. There are some simple fixes for these situations, but they won't just go away without addressing them!

8. <u>Brush our teeth</u> after every time we eat, if at all possible! At the least, we brush in the morning after breakfast and in the evening after our last food at night. Leaving food bits in our mouth and teeth when we sleep makes a super breeding ground for bacteria and results in decay. It doesn't do nice things for our breath, either! Yecch! So we brush – and floss – and get all that stuff out from between our teeth. Sometimes bad breath simply comes from old food particles left between the teeth – an easy fix with dental floss. For pleasant breath, healthy teeth and gums, daily flossing is an important habit to develop! (Of course, we need to see a dentist on a regular basis, so our teeth can be their best for our entire life.)

9. <u>Remember that *hands tell a tale*</u> – and not always what we intend! If they are dirty and if there is *crud* under the nails, it's just a turn-off – and unhygienic, besides! So, we keep our hands clean, use a nail brush when needed (they're cheap to buy and easily found at drug stores and markets), use a nail file to smooth rough nails and we *nip* hangnails with cuticle nippers or tiny manicure scissors. We don't tear or bite off hangnails – ouch!

If we bite our nails, we try to stop. It is possible! One good way (a tip for both guys and gals) to help stop this habit, is to take care of rough or broken spots on nails right away. Keep a nail file/emery board/nail smoother handy and use it! It will help to keep our nails out of our mouth so we won't *worry* them back to the quick or feel the need to *groom* the snags and broken bits with our teeth. Having small successes with keeping our nails snag-free can also help us to be more aware of the possibilities of having nicer, longer nails. If we can leave them alone more, our nails *will* soon start to show noticeable growth.

10. <u>Pay attention to clothes selection</u>. Picking out what's appropriate and what looks good together for a given situation doesn't come naturally to everyone. Some young women are great at this, and some young men are gifted with being able to create a sharp look. Wherever a person falls in this spectrum of *clothing cool*, we can give a thought to colors that work together and to looking at ourselves from all angles when we're trying on clothes! The *sit test* and the *bend-over test* are handy checks to see if we keep covered those body parts best left to the imagination! Clothes that fit always look better than clothes that look skimpy or show inappropriate or distracting skin or undergarments. Well-fitting clothing is more flattering no matter our weight or body-shape. So, we use those mirrors and take a look at our selections – from the back and the sides as well. And, our clothes selections don't have to be expensive; *great looks* can happen on small budgets!

Now, our Big Two – our clinchers for satisfying first impressions and for presenting ourselves in all the moments thereafter:

Ta-dah!
We wear a SMILE
We have a POSITIVE ATTITUDE

Our Big Two, a smile and a positive attitude, give depth and quality to all the other nice things we do to present ourselves. They make our efforts work for us and click into place! Without these two, any first impression is a shallow thing; a fleeting presentation moment of "Look at me!"

Nothing is more welcoming and attractive than a simple smile! It can say so much about us without a word. It can instantly help put others at ease – always a kind, good thing! A smile on our face makes *the best* first impression!

And a positive attitude certainly helps to create a lasting excellent impression! *Our positive attitude transforms our every moment;* it makes us someone people want to get to know!

We elaborate a lot more on the power of a smile and a positive attitude in our chapter 15: *Clothes Don't Make the Young Woman or Man – But a Smile Sure Does!* and in chapter 7, *An Attitude of Gratitude (The magic of living in thankfulness – and the antidote to "I'm bored!")*.

We Can Always Ask for Assistance!
If it seems that we have skin or teeth or other health or grooming challenges, there are professionals out there to help. For each of us, there is someone who could be a resource for getting answers to our large or small questions and who could lead us in a helpful direction. Trusted family members and friends often are great places to start our networking to the healthful, happy self-presentation we desire!

In addition, professional, valid sites online can often provide information and suggestions for better health choices. Several of those to check out would be: www.choosemyplate.gov/

www.tuftshealthletter.com/

www.hsph.harvard.edu/nutritionsource/

Not to Be Missed!
This chapter has an especially useful, idea-packed section at the end! By taking a look at our *Opportunities for Consideration and Practice* and by considering some of the suggestions found there, we can further discover that:

Small Steps Help Make Better Days!

When we boil it down, all this first impression and daily presentation stuff is, at its simplest, a kindly gesture – of self-respect!

And when we take small steps to present who we are *inside* with a clean, caring and pleasant *outside*, we not only show respect for ourselves, but also for those around us and for our daily comings-and-goings!

This attitude of caring can help form our days into really good, satisfying ones. It is another example of *The Etiquette of Kindness* in action!

So each day, in easy, basic ways, we can help ourselves feel more confident in how we look and how we feel – how we present ourselves to our *public!*

After all, no matter how shy or introverted or how bubbly or extroverted we may be, each one of us likes to feel that confident *"Ta-dah!"* moment inside!

Consideration and Practice Opportunities:

Go back into this chapter; take a look at the various sections there and pick out any that you'd like to consider for yourself. As an individual, as a family or as a class, think about possibilities for creating generally better health, greater self-confidence and better first – and lasting – impressions.

<u>Personally</u> –

Perhaps re-read the section: Our *Top Ten* – Plus the Big Two! Look down our list there and see if there's anything you'd like to consider in *upping* the quality of your personal care. For instance...

<u>A radiant smile!</u>

Do you take as good care of your teeth as you might?

- If not, make it a practice to floss and brush at least twice a day. Start with a week of excellent dental care – then add another and another…and see your smile *shine!*

- If you haven't seen your dentist in some time, make arrangements to do so – then follow any advice that she or he has for you.

Clothes we're proud to wear!

Do you take pains to wear neat and clean clothes and to repair any (non-*fashionable)* tears or replace missing buttons?

- If there is room for improvement here, take a week and go through your closet or drawers and attend to what needs fixing.

- If you find you don't wear items of clothing because they look "sad" and not sharp without ironing, take a couple of hours, put on some music and iron away! You'll probably feel pretty happy knowing that those clothes you've been avoiding – but love! – are now hanging up, just waiting to be worn!

- Or, if you find you really can't stand the prospect of ironing, but know you won't like the way you look in some items without touching them up, consider donating those pieces of clothing to someone who could use them. (And, in future clothes buying take a look at fabric care tags and perhaps give the hem of any garment you're considering the crumple test in your hand. If it crumples and wrinkles easily and you don't like that look, don't buy – or be ready to iron!)

- Then, make it a routine to keep your clothing in better repair and nicely presentable – *as* you go along; this will only add positively to your self confidence.

What are our hands (and feet) expressing?

What about your hands and feet? What "story" are they telling about your personal cleanliness and care habits? Are you proud of how they look, or is there room for improvement? If you believe you could stand some upgrading in this personal care department, take a week and allocate that period to better habits of care and cleanliness.

- If you need a pumice stone or callus smoother, cuticle nippers, a nail brush or file, make those small purchases – then use them! Be proud of how much nicer your hands, feet and nails look!

- Perhaps go and get a manicure or pedicure so you know better how to take care of your hands and feet and their nails. Or, get the advice and help of a knowledgeable friend or relative who would just love to help you learn nail care.

- If you bite your nails, look into how to stop this detracting habit – and then go about making this change. (It can be done!)

<u>As an individual or as a family –</u>

Turn back a few pages in our chapter here and take another look at our section, *Get the Good Fuel Our Body Craves – and Thrives On!* This section is a great one for considering both our own personal food and beverage choices, as well as making better nutrition a family project!

As a family or as an individual, perhaps take a week or two – or a month – and concentrate on improving beverage choices, drinking more water, eating a nutritious breakfast everyday or making a big effort to add more veggies and whole fruits to your daily menu. Talk about this and develop a plan! After the agreed-upon time period, check back in on how your plan went. Discuss successes and challenges.

<u>Water! (And other liquids!)</u>

To help get you started in looking and feeling your best, consider the hints in *Get the Good Fuel Our Body Craves – and Thrives On!* For instance when it comes to beverages:

- If drinking "buckets" of soda is a habit, you might make a decision to cut back to one or two soda drinks a day – or to *none*, if you prefer, or your health care provider advises.

- Substitute sodas with 100% real fruit, non-sugar-added juices — preferably diluted by about half with plain or sparkling water. Add ice, if you like and enjoy!

- If it's been a habit to *begin* your day with a soda, work on eliminating that one first, eating a better, non sugar-laden breakfast selected from protein, fruits and whole grains to help fuel your brain!

- Increase your plain water drinking to about eight tall glasses (*at least* 8 oz. per glass) a day — more if you are sweating a lot or doing heavy exercise or sports in any weather! (This is an excellent practice anyway, whether you drink any sodas or not.)

- Avoid so-called "energy drinks"! Basically, no matter how the ads and the commercials try to glamorize and sell you these liquids, gulping down heavy doses of caffeine, sugars and other herbs and elements meant to give us a temporary, artificial "hit" of nervous energy is *not* a good thing! Rely on enough sleep, exercise, plenty of water, good foods (beginning with a nutritious, non-sugary breakfast, please), time outdoors and choosing a positive, grateful attitude, to get *energized and high on Life!*

- If you have any questions as to *why* you should consider cutting way back or eliminating soda drinks and why you should not choose so-called *energy drinks*, ask your doctor, dentist, nutritionist or other health professional.

<u>Champion food choices!</u>

Additionally, for our better health, more vital energy, mental alertness and to help us look our best we certainly want to consider:

- Cutting out or way back on any deep-fried foods, like yummy-tasting French fries, many *fast foods,* donuts and chips! Reserve these and all "fast foods" as *treats* and enjoy *on occasion.*

- If fresh veggies and fruits have gone begging in your daily food choices, plan on upping your intake of these health and beauty-giving foods!

- Eat a good, nutritious, non-sugary breakfast, consisting of selections such as eggs, yogurt, cheese, whole grain toast, fruits, seeds and nuts, whole grain hot or cold cereals (with little or no sugar added).

- Become a label reader! If seeking better health, looking and feeling your best is important, read labels of all the foods that come packaged, before you buy! Take a look at the sugar and fat contents and at the ingredients that go into the food or *food product*. Ask your doctor, nurse practitioner, nutritionist or go online (see our suggestions on page 194 for reliable websites to try) to seek general knowledge about food ingredients and current suggestions for fats and sugars in our daily food choices.

Snack-a-licious!

Great, more healthful snack selections might be:

- Crisp carrots, broccoli "flowers", cucumber slices, cross-cut celery "bites", jicama and sweet pepper slices – with or without delicious and good-for-you hummus or perhaps *a bit* (a tablespoon or so) of ranch dressing for dipping – yum!

- For another crunchy snack, enjoy air-popped pop corn with little or no butter and no, or just a dash of, salt or seasoned salt! This can easily substitute for those deep-fried, salt-laden chips.

- One or two granola-type or oatmeal cookies on occasion. These could be gluten-free or made with whole grain flours; they could be lower sugar, perhaps sweetened with honey and packed with good-for-us seeds and nuts, along with bits of dried fruits – and "even" a few chocolate chips thrown in for good measure!

- Yogurt, either with fruit already added or add your own blueberries, strawberries or raspberries and perhaps some granola, if you like that – delicious!

- Apple slices, banana slices or celery sticks paired with peanut or other nut or seed butter.

- Fresh mandarins or other oranges — bits of sunshine in your hand!

Getting Help and Info —

As mentioned earlier in our chapter, in any areas of health and personal development where we may feel unsure or need info, we can get assistance! There are often skilled and knowledgeable adult friends and family members who can assist us or who would be happy to steer us to health and esthetic professionals. All are glad to help us feel good and achieve greater self-confidence!

And, clarifying info on health, nutrition and wellness subjects can often be found online at sites of *trusted government or medical institutions.* (See our several suggestions in this chapter, under the heading: *We Can Always Ask for Assistance!)* Some of the articles found on those sites, written by health professionals, are easily understood and can be truly helpful!

Outside!

What about getting outside and enjoying the benefits and pure fun of Nature? As an individual or as a family or class, do you do this enough — at least some every day or most days?

- If not, consider dedicating a week or two to "unplugging" from any electronics for an hour or two. Go outside to take a walk, play, stretch, shoot some hoops, work in the garden, throw a ball, hike, go for a swim or run, bike, sled, skate or row...

- Whatever you might enjoy and whatever your particular level of health and ability allows — DO it!

- Then, after this week or longer of outdoor immersion, take stock! Have you had moments or hours of joy and adventure that you might not have had without this new outdoors perspective and experience? Have you perhaps found an increase in your general happiness and brightness of thinking — more positivity, better physical energy, perhaps?

- Consider making going outside a daily – or most days – habit! Nature is our wonderful friend and its benefits can make us all feel more vital, more alive – more fully, outstandingly *ourselves!* Nature's here for us in all its "Ta-dah!" glory! From reaffirming sunrises through gorgeous sunsets and starry skies, it's all a reminder of our natural links to the fabulous goodness, beauty and abundance of our earth. It's a pure health and beauty-providing *gift* – enjoy some every day!

Check Back!

When you, your family or your class have completed your dedicated period of making better food and beverage choices and of actively getting outside nearly every day, check in on how it all went!

Consider for yourself or talk about together, any improvements in how you feel mentally and in how you look and feel physically.

Good things to consider might be:

Is your skin clearer and more glowing?

Having made a nutritious breakfast a daily habit, are you finding that you think sharper in the morning and right on through to lunchtime?

Were you outside, moving, playing and exercising most days?

Do you look and feel trimmer (maybe the scales show this as well)?

Do you feel generally more alert and more even, mentally?

Are there any increases in feeling happier?

Did you successfully increase your water drinking throughout each day?

How did it go with making more healthful snack choices and what were some that you particularly enjoyed?

<u>*Ta-dah!* A good morning greeting!</u>

Here's a really simple, uplifting habit to get into for beginning every day from a happier, more outgoing perspective:

> Each morning, *just by yourself,* go outside to greet the day — acknowledge it and give thanks! Sniff the air; take a big breath; bend and stretch! See what the day feels like and what it may have in store. This is a Life-affirming, positive way to begin any day! Consider making these few, private and peaceful moments of greeting the morning a lifetime habit. Enjoy!
>
> Note: "Outside" can be *any version of fresh air in Nature that is available* to you. From an open window in a city, to an apartment balcony, a condo patio, a small or large backyard, a city park, a country hilltop, an expanse of rolling farmland, a lakeshore, a mountaintop… However and wherever we can look out, step out or venture out into Nature, even for a few minutes, gives us a chance to re-set, widen our perspective on Life and get grounded for the coming day! This is too good to miss! Treat yourself!

<u>There's nothing like it!</u>

In our chapter 7, *An Attitude of Gratitude (The magic of living in thankfulness — and the antidote to "I'm bored!"),* lies a *treasure* for improving our first (and *all!*) impressions. Consider taking another look at that chapter, because —

> Gratitude — and the positive attitude that naturally comes with it — helps us to bloom as full, kindly and compassionate, *stand-out* human beings with every reason to say "Ta-dah!"

And, always remember our very simple and super easy basic: *all* first impressions are made immeasurably better with a welcoming, friendly smile!

15.

Clothes Don't Make The Young Woman Or Man

A Smile Sure Does!

With so much concern and attention out there these days on "What to wear?" or on what other people are wearing or about how we (or others!) look, it's sometimes easy to get lost in appearances!

It's very good to remember that we can look wonderful in clothing that is clean, attractive, appropriate and perhaps modest in cost — yet *rich* in *"okayness"*!

And, as we mentioned in chapter 14, *Ta-dah! First Impressions,* a SMILE is key to our *presentation,* and a smile is *the* very best thing to wear (of course, along with other appropriate apparel)!

A smile almost always indicates graciousness, openness, welcome, kindness. We know, of course, that occasionally life includes some tough experiences making a smile difficult or perhaps not even appropriate or possible in the moment during the truly hard times.

The Mighty Power of a Smile!

If we find ourselves at times just *feeling down or* feeling sorry for ourselves or not too friendly (it happens to all of us!), we probably really don't want to *slop all over others* with our bad attitude. We undoubtedly would like to change any sourness or gloom we are feeling. Sometimes we can begin our attitude adjustment by *faking it* for a moment with a smile we at first think we don't mean, but one that can grow on us and take us by surprise!

Since a smile of any sort is powerful, we can use this initially pasted-on, created smile to get us kick-started in a new direction – until its mighty facial-and-attitude-adjusting *power* can take over our brains and hearts and lead us in a better direction!

We can take this handy step to a better, more positive thought pattern even when we are alone and feeling not too nice and anti-social, or when we are just laboring under the considerable weight of self-absorbed oppressive thinking.

The Smile Transformation Tool

Here's what we do:

> First we just turn up the corners of our mouth.

> We get that settled in and flex it a few times.

> Then we take that smile up into our eyes. (We can feel that happening!)

Voilà! This physical facial change can *start* the process of lifting our spirits as if by magic.

For our purposes, we won't waste any time nor feelings of anxiety on thinking we're *being a fake* or insincere! This *pasting on of a smile* is just a tool for attitude change, much as actors use tools to get themselves into character for the roles they play. Our desired role in this instance is that of the happier person we enjoy being and a pasted-on-for-the-moment-smile is a good tool to help us get back into the real, kindly character of ourselves!

Then We Mindfully Add Gratitude!

Of course, as we learned together in chapter 7, *An Attitude of Gratitude,* the key to solidly lifting our attitude is our kindly reminding ourselves of the true transforming magic of gratitude! We turn our attention to thankfulness in the large and small aspects of the life which we enjoy, with the result that our willingness of heart and our action of thinking out from thanks-giving put a real, sincere smile on our face!

With a gratitude-based transforming smile, we are now ready to use the skills we've learned so well in our *Etiquette of Kindness!*

Practice and Discussion Opportunities:

Go back to each of the three sub-headings in our chapter here. Re-read them and plan an entire day when you will take these tips and try to do them. This can be done just on your own, or as a family, with friends or as a class "project" or *smiling experiment!*

> Pay attention to what happens when you remember to smile — even if you think you *don't mean it* at first.

> If you are doing this practice with others, when the experiment is over (the day or several days; whatever you decided) get together and discuss what happened for each of you. Tell how you felt. Share observations and any interesting results that you feel were directly connected to your *smiling experiment!*

Plan to, in the future, make this not just an experiment, but a regular good habit and tool to turn your attitude and your days into more positive, happier ones. It works!

16.

That Summer Job

A job can be a fun and satisfying experience!

Whether for a few days or a few months, part time or full time, whether large or small, any job is an opportunity for us to learn and to expand a variety of skills. With a job, we can practice good time management, flex our creative talents, enjoy interactions with others and strengthen habits of reliability and responsibility.

Every job we will have in our life will benefit from the positive approaches and good habits that we learn and practice – now!

And *all* jobs are opportunities to practice our Etiquette of Kindness skills and courtesies!

It Begins with the Presentation!
Our handling of every job is important, so there's no such thing as "*just* going to the neighbors to mow their lawn" or "*just* going out to wash the neighbors'

car" or "*only* going down the road to do my horse feeding job!" Every time we go out in public, how we present ourselves shows our level of self-respect and our attitude of caring. It is an indicator of the thoroughness and appreciation we bring to our tasks. Presenting ourselves neatly, cleanly and appropriately dressed for the activity is a pleasure for others to behold and instills confidence in employers!

Whether our summer job is walking and feeding the neighbors' dogs, babysitting little kids, raking yards and cutting grass, doing housecleaning, feeding horses, being a mother's helper or selling our home-grown veggies at the local farmers' market, how we present ourselves counts! No matter what our job is, we'll want to incorporate these basics:

- We wash our face, brush our teeth and comb our hair every day before leaving the house — even to go next door to do a job for a neighbor!

- We put on clean and appropriate clothing for the task we'll be doing.

- We eat a healthful, adequate (NOT sugar-laden!) breakfast so our brain can think clearly and our emotions can have a better chance at staying on an even keel!

- We begin our days by practicing our Attitude of Gratitude which immediately helps us to smile and to act and think positively!

- We use the skills we've learned about speaking to others and looking them in the eyes when we say "Hello!" and when we converse.

- We remember our good phone and e-communication skills and courtesies.

- We think to use the simple but thoughtful words "Please!" "Thank you!" and "May I?" in our dealings with others — it's appreciated!

Get the Info!

For any job, we make sure to get all the necessary information. We find out *who, what, where, when and how* and then we *write it down or enter the info in our phone or other electronic device.* We leave nothing to our memory! In this way, we won't end up embarrassed by a lack of needed information. We won't miss what we have agreed to do.

We make notes of the following:

- *Who* our employer is – and the name of anyone else with whom we will be involved.

- *What* the job is – what will be expected of us; what we will need to accomplish.

- *Where* we need to be – and any special directions.

- *When* we need to be there – and how often if the job is for more than a single time.

- *How* we will do the job – and will we need or desire to bring our own tools or special items such as a hat, sunscreen, gloves, etc. (For yard work, do we bring our own equipment? If we are cleaning someone's house, do we bring anything of our own to do the job? If we are babysitting, do we have special books or craft items we want to share with the children?)

Target Time!

Here's an important (possibly life-changing and job-saving) tip to help keep us on time in all we do: When we need to be somewhere at a specific time, we should consider any *prep time* we'll need and figure in any *travel time* to get to our destination. We use those facts for figuring our timing. That becomes our all-important *Target Time*. For example:

> We need to be at the stable a few miles away at 5:00 p.m. for our summer job of stable cleaning and horse walking. We ride our bike to our stable job every afternoon, all summer long.

> Riding at a pretty good but easy, safe pace, it takes right at 30 minutes to make the trip. Since we like to get there early just to visit and see

what's up, we add about 15 minutes to the 30 minutes and this is now our *travel time*. That means our *Target Time* for leaving is 4:15!

We *think 4:15* (NOT 5:00) in everything we do regarding scheduling our other activities and being ready for and getting to our job – right up until we hop on our bike!

We also need to change into our stable clothes and grab a snack at home. Those two things together take about 15 minutes to do – our *Prep Time*. So, with a *Target Time* for leaving at 4:15, we know that by 4:00 we should be dressed, fixing and eating our snack, ready to leave at 4:15 p.m.

We arrive a bit early and in plenty of time for our job at 5:00, feeling happy, friendly, peaceful, confident and *together!*

For wherever we need to be or for whatever project we need to accomplish at a certain time, we can make everything come together well and on time when we

- note our needed *Job/Appointment/Event/Project Date and Time;*

- figure our *Prep Time* (whatever time it will take us to be ready for our job, appointment, event or project);

- figure any needed *Travel Time* in normal circumstances, plus some extra, for getting to our destination, whether we are walking, biking, driving;

- consider allowing more time for the *Unknowns* in either our prep or our travel time (Those *unexpecteds* happen!);

- begin any needed travel at our *Target Time*.

Thoughtfully considering and allocating our time in this way works for creating success with being on time for appointments, for projects and for events!

Our Prep Time can be minutes, hours, a few or many days.

Our Travel Time can be none (if, for instance, we are responsible for something happening at home), or it can be minutes, hours or, in the case of a big trip, days.

It works! We will be on time or even early! In any case, we will be unapologetic, relaxed, cheerful and ready to fulfill our job.

We Don't Agree to the Impossible to Try to Please Others!

Here's another very important consideration in making logical and peaceful use of Time.

It can be tempting to try to do the impossible to please our friends, or, in speaking here of jobs, to please an employer or prospective employer. Sometimes, we will agree to be someplace at a certain time, though, if we really think about what we are committing to, we'll realize it's humanly impossible! In agreeing without figuring in all the timing, we are setting ourselves up for failure, disappointment, embarrassment — and for others to be irritated with us!

> *Jaimie* has a new yard care business he's trying to get going, working after school and weekends. He is really excited to get a call from *Mr. Chambers* who lives a few blocks away. Jaimie has hoped that Mr. Chambers would want to employ him for weeding and cutting his lawns, and here's his opportunity to get started!
>
> Mr. Chambers says he'd like for Jaimie to meet him at his house in one half hour, advising Jaimie that punctuality is really important to him. Wanting very much to please Mr. Chambers and to secure the job, he agrees to the meeting in half an hour, though he's just sat down to breakfast his mom cooked, still in his p.j.'s and will need to ride his bike over to the Chambers', a solid ten-minute ride.
>
> Jaimie gobbles down his breakfast, throws on some clothes, doesn't take time to brush his teeth, runs his fingers through his hair, hops on his bike, pedals like crazy, realizes he's running late, is nervous and upset — and arrives at Mr. Chambers' house almost ten minutes

late. Mr. Chambers greets the apologetic, sweating and miserable Jaimie. He feels that it's necessary to lecture Jaimie on the importance of being on time if he's going to work for his family and throws in something about how he values reliability and punctuality. Jaimie is embarrassed and feels physically and emotionally exhausted, though Mr. Chambers ultimately gives him the job of his lawn care — IF he can be on time.

Logic, Target Time and the Possible!

What might Jaimie have done differently to not end up in this miserable situation? When his prospective employer asked for the half-hour time frame, Jaimie could have thought about it a bit and determined what *was* possible. Jaimie would have looked at the facts logically, taking into consideration his needed prep and travel time, giving him a *possible*, doable *Target Time!* He would have then courteously offered that meeting time to Mr. Chambers.

Let's look at this little scenario again:

> Jaimie gets a call from Mr. Chambers, who would like to have Jaimie meet him at his house in half an hour to discuss the possibility of Jaimie's doing their lawn care. Jaimie's first inclination is to please Mr. Chambers by agreeing, even if the initial requested meeting time is impossible for him to fulfill. But he takes a few seconds to think about it and realizes that he can't accomplish meeting that half-hour time request. He knows that it will take him at least ten minutes to eat the breakfast his mom has prepared, at least fifteen minutes to brush his teeth, shower and dress and at least ten minutes to make the bike ride over, putting him at the Chambers' five or maybe ten minutes late for what Mr. Chambers is asking.

> Jaimie has learned that he can only do what is possible — even when it comes to pleasing his friends, family and prospective employers! So, he says to Mr. Chambers:

> "Thank you so much for calling me, Mr. Chambers! I am excited to discuss what you need at your place and how I can help out! It's 8:30 now. It'll take me forty-five minutes to finish what I'm doing here

and bike to your house. I can see you at 9:15. Will that work okay for you?"

Mr. Chambers agrees. Jaimie eats breakfast without ridiculously stuffing himself, thanks his mom, showers and otherwise gets himself together to meet his prospective employer and calmly bikes over to the house, easily arriving a couple of minutes early! Mr. Chambers and he greet each other and have a pleasant conversation. Mr. Chambers finds no reason to lecture or reprimand. Jaimie doesn't suffer miserably through embarrassment brought on by agreeing to the impossible! They are off to a good start and Jaimie gets the job!

Setting up for Success!
So! Much as we might like to fulfill someone's request, we are realists! When it comes to trying to please others, we don't agree to the impossible, setting ourselves up for failure and embarrassment. Instead, we set ourselves up for success!

- We figure what *is* possible and proceed from that point of reality!

- We are calm, collected, happy and self-confident when we agree to the possible!

- We bring this happy, peaceful confidence to our interactions with friends, family, employers and to all whom we meet.

- We work hard in any task or undertaking we have agreed to do.

- We do our very best!

- We end up being truly pleasing to others when we *agree to the possible!*

Every Job Counts!
That old saying, "Any job worth doing, is worth doing well," is so true!

When we take up a task, we do it well and thoroughly, ultimately taking pride in its skillful completion.

We bring this attitude and will force to any job we do – including our summer or part time jobs. These count as *real* jobs! They can be fun, adventurous, skill-enhancing and income-producing experiences. They can take us to different places and help us to meet new, interesting people. Every job gives us more opportunities to practice thoroughness, timeliness, courtesy, thoughtfulness – and all of the aspects of our Etiquette of Kindness. Yaay! Go, us!

Practice and Consideration Opportunities:

Go back to the second heading, *Target Time,* in our chapter here. Re-read that one as well as the next two, *We Don't Agree to the Impossible…*and *Logic, Target Time and the Possible.*

> Set aside one week to zero in on using these hints for success in your timing and in your agreements with others. Whether or not you have an outside job, a job around the house, a homework or other assignment or if you are committed to do any small or large fun or worthwhile thing with someone, apply these principles to every agreement or appointment for this week.

> Be mindful of how thoroughly you do this.

> When the week is over, sit down and think back on how it all went.

> > Were you more successful with your timing than usual?

> > Did you get the full information so that you could commit knowledgably to agreements, appointments or deadlines – setting yourself up for success?

> > Were you able to see improvements in meeting your agreements and commitments?

Did you feel any relaxation of anxiety that you might usually experience when under pressure of meeting appointments or deadlines? Were you more peaceful?

Did you experience any increased sense of personal dignity; were you proud of how you approached all your time commitments?

Give yourself a huge pat on the back, if you were able to make the dedication to being more time and agreement successful for this week!

If you know you didn't do this thoroughly, get re-focused! Go back and re-read this small chapter again. Take special note of what you may have left out of your plan for success with your timing: Did you forget to carefully assess the scope of the job, agreement or assignment? Did you agree, either with another person or with yourself (for example, if you were trying to bring a homework assignment in on time), to a time frame that wasn't logical and doable? Did you kid yourself or were you trying to please someone, when what you agreed to just couldn't be done in the time you allotted?

Select a week in the near future and go at it again – this time, do your very best and work hard at this, as if achieving successful *Target Time* is a job itself, which you need to complete well. Keep at it! Your success with this will give you increased self confidence and poise; it will set you up for greater success in all you undertake – it makes for a great beginning to all endeavors and agreements! Good going, everyone!

17.

Nobody's Perfect!

Or
What to Do When We Mess Up!
(Because it will happen!)

No matter how hard we try, there are times when we *mess up!*

As human beings, each of us has instances when we feel — or *know* — that we have messed up!

Occasionally we forget something we shouldn't, or we actually hurt someone's feelings or are thoughtless or shockingly unkind. Yikes!

It happens.

We can mess up *privately* when we are thinking meanly or judgmentally. But, since (for good or for ill) our thoughts color our actions, words and deeds, unless we realize what we are doing, *get a grip* and turn them around, our private imperfections of heart and mind don't remain just our own personal misery. Nope! Courtesy of our mean-spirited and narrow perspective, they end up *out there* impacting others! Misery added to misery!

Thankfully however, Life is a group effort! We are not on our own here to flounder around; we are all learning and growing together – and *no* one of us is *perfect!*

And, we can be glad that our imperfections definitely can have some redeeming upsides! Yes, it's true: if we use them as learning tools, our mistakes provide us opportunities for expanding our humility, discernment, determination and creativity. They provide plenty of occasions for increasing our kindness, understanding, compassion and forgiveness.

It's a good thing, indeed, that as we go along in our day-to-day living, we sometimes look back through our rear-view mirror of Life and ask ourselves:

"*What* was I thinking?"

The view we get with this backwards perspective (also famously called *hindsight*) of years, months or days can occasionally shock us! From our perspective today of what we've come to realize as responsible and thoughtful, we wonder "*How* could I *ever* have been that shallow, that unkind, that thoughtless, that foolish, that mean, that…?" (Any of these descriptions of poor qualities could probably apply to most of us at one time or another!)

That's to be expected, since:

• We all *flub up* from time to time, and sometimes *big time.*

• We have a conscience!

• We care, and because we care, we learn.

- We figure out the better choices and approaches – and we go on to do better, to make wiser and kinder choices.

Kindness and Consideration Today Creates Kinder Tomorrows!

When we learn from our decisions and hold them up to our basic value of kindness – of treating others as we'd want to be treated in similar circumstances – our *future* backward-looking can hold fewer embarrassed and sorry "Oh, my!"'s and more moments of which we can be proud!

After all, since we're not here alone and since Life is a group effort, doing our part to create kinder, happier moments and days is a very good reason to be learning – and practicing – the skills of The Etiquette of Kindness together!

First Step to Reset: *Gratitude!*

Since we all basically want to be happy – and want to return to happiness when we realize we've done something to make us and others unhappy, there's good, simple news and a ready first step for when we *mess up*:

It's that old *attitude of gratitude* again! We can be *grateful!*

Wow, really? Grateful?

Yes! Gratitude is the key to starting the turn-around to happiness: gratitude that we realize what we've done and have the skills and humility to do better and to begin again in greater awareness and happiness!

We are grateful that we know the difference between how we've acted, spoken, thought or judged in a situation or toward another person and how we want to act, speak, think and feel. That positive emotion of gratitude – gratitude that we *know better* – will take us to our ultimate step of *doing better* in our thinking, acting, speaking. In fact, we'll find ourselves doing better in the very next moment…and in the moments after that…and after that!

Next Step: *Apology!*

From gratitude for our realization that we should, want to and can *do better,* it's an easy next step to *apology!*

Sometimes, our *mess-up* is just a personal, private one: we realize that we are judging (again – sigh!) or thinking meanly. In this case, we can privately *apologize* to ourselves and resolve to immediately begin again: thinking – and thereby acting – in a better spirit of kindness!

If however our unhappy mess-up in our thinking, speaking or acting has taken on a *public face* – if others are offended or impacted by what we've done or said – then the next step is easy to identify: we need to *apologize!*

- We sincerely state what we realize we've done.

- We sincerely say how sorry we are.

- We hope for forgiveness and understanding, whether it is given or not.

- We then go on to do better right now and in the future.

For instance:

We're at a gathering of our family and friends; we are having a problem with our thinking and attitude today. Maybe we just *feel mean* and have forgotten to use our ever-handy, true and simple *attitude of gratitude* to help get ourselves out of this foul mood and back into *happy* – or *happy-enough!*

Unfortunately, while everyone else is laughing and enjoying being together, we act on our mean-spirited *down mood* and say something ugly and unkind. We can tell that this has put a wet blanket on the gathering – at least for those people who heard our not-so-nice comments. We don't like this dark, icky feeling inside or the not-so-nice, hurt responses we are getting!

So, if we've lashed out *just because we could* and hurt people's feelings or ruined the moment in some way, then as soon as we realize what we've done:

- We stop.

- We change our attitude.

- We are *grateful* that we can change our attitude and improve our future actions.

- We apologize clearly and appropriately.

- We then *quietly move on* in kindness in our thoughts, words and actions — the truest, greatest apology when we've messed up!

Our Apologies Aren't Always Accepted, But...

We are grateful for others' courtesy and kindness in accepting our apology, but we don't *worry* about whether others accept our apology or not; that's their business. Each of us is on our own journey of figuring out how we act and what we do with our feelings.

Everyone does the best with what skills and awareness she or he has at any time. Most people realize that they, too, are not *perfect*. They appreciate the humility it takes to apologize; they value the mutual healing opportunity a sincere apology can bring. They are glad to accept our apology — and to go forward in greater peace and happiness!

So, we apologize in sincerity — no matter the reaction. We move on *with gratitude* that we can begin again and do better — and we do just that!

And When We Forget — or Just *Procrastinate* Into Total Embarrassment?

Sometimes, we out-and-out forget something. At other times, we just seem to keep getting in our own way of behaving as we know we want to — and as we should! And, as we keep putting off what we need to take care of, our delay — our procrastination — compounds our misery and our embarrassment!

If we just put off things we know we should take care of, we might find ourselves in a situation similar to this:

Aunt Alice sent us a birthday gift and we totally forgot (or procrastinated!) about thanking her — and it's now been a couple of months. Yikes! Maybe the book she sent we've already read or the sweater (which we actually liked a lot) we wore often or the game she sent us we've played a number of times — without taking care of thanking her. Unkind! Embarrassing! What to do?

Easy! We say "Thank you!" *now!*

But first thing, incorporated into our thanks, we apologize for being so late in doing so! Here's a possible example for a note – handwritten and sent through the mail, please! We won't use short-cuts with e-mail, a phone call or a text, especially at *this* late date:

"Dear Aunt Alice –

How could I have neglected to thank you for that great sweater you sent to me for my birthday? I love it! I've worn it often!

I am so sorry that I didn't just sit down and write you my thanks! I certainly should have just done it – I thought of it a number of times but, somehow, I just didn't get it done.

Then, it got so late that I got more and more embarrassed. But I finally realized that I wanted to thank you and let you know I appreciated your thoughtfulness more than I wanted to live with my embarrassment – or with you undoubtedly thinking that I didn't like your gift or didn't appreciate your thoughtfulness! Please accept my apology – and my thanks, Aunt Alice!

Thank you for your kindness in remembering me – and for selecting something that is perfect! I love the color. I love the style. I get compliments on it every time I wear it."

This is the idea, no matter the gift, kindness or situation: we are sincere and we don't waste anymore time in embarrassment over our procrastination! Once we remember to take care of thanking *Aunt Alice* (or anyone else), we just get on it and make it sincere and interesting. (More on this in our chapter 6, *"Thank you!" Writing Letters and Notes...*)

Those Embarrassing Little *Yikes Moments!*
Even something as simple as introductions can be an occasion for catching ourselves in the moment of a *mess-up.*

Say we're introducing our friend to other friends – and we suddenly *space* on our friend's name! Yikes!

The very best thing is to just own up to this *yikes moment* and say something like: "Wow! I can't believe it! My mind just went blank with my best friend's name!"

Hopefully, our friend will just laugh it off and immediately come to our aid with, "Oh, Mike, for goodness sake — *Jessica!*" Then, with some good humor, some laughter and agreement that this happens, we and our friends go on to an even better, more comfortable and successful introduction and conversation experience!

Always, it's the best to:

- be *real;*

- be *sincere;*

- *own up* to any little (and large!) mistakes;

- *realize* that we are not alone, that everyone messes up occasionally;

- *smile!*

Actually, when we acknowledge the fact of our humanity, it helps everyone to *relax* and to be *kinder.*

(See chapter 3, *Making Your Acquaintance! Meeting and Greeting...*)

Oh, My Gosh!

Okay, here's another possibility: we forgot to meet our friend for lunch — just totally spaced on it — or we put it on the wrong day on our calendar or we never made a note of it at all! What do we do? We call to tell him or her how very sorry we are! We pick up the phone or write a text/e-mail — whichever way we know our friend will get the message sooner. Then, if there's any doubt about making contact, we follow up to make certain we've communicated!

So, we apologize and then perhaps we and our friend make plans to get together in the future. We make certain that we both understand the plan, the place, day and time. Then, we thank our friend for being so kind and understanding. (We are assuming in our example here that our friend will take this approach and kindly *give us a break,* accepting our apology with good nature.)

One of us might even pick up the phone or text or e-mail the day before, or several hours prior, to remind the other of our plans. It never hurts to help each other make good things happen!

Opportunities!

As we can see, even in those times when we mess up (and it *will* happen), honesty and directness are the way to go!

We can step up to a situation, *grateful* that we recognize what we need to do to turn it around or to try to mend it.

With this approach, when we take any needed steps to apologize, even painful, awkward events can often become opportunities for greater understanding, wisdom, humility and compassion; for insightful humor, deeper friendship and true forgiveness.

Our missteps and imperfections can become *perfect* opportunities for developing our Etiquette of Kindness! After all, nobody's perfect!

Contemplation and Practice Opportunities:

Go back in this chapter and re-read our section, *And When We Forget — or Just Procrastinate Into Total Embarrassment?* Contemplate if there are any "loose ends" of thanks or apology that you *know* need to be taken care of; things that you realized at the time — or later — that you should have done differently, or for which you never took the time to make a proper thanks or acknowledgment. Do it now! Take a few minutes and write the thank you note you "owe"; pick up the phone and let someone know that you are sorry; write or call and let a person know that you have been thinking of them and that you care — even if she or he hasn't heard from you for some time!

Any time is a good time to take care of things we've left undone or apologies we might owe! You will feel better about yourself and about the situation and the recipient of your care will benefit, as well! Being remembered, acknowledged and valued is always a good thing!

18.

Kindness Has A Long History!

We are in excellent company in learning skills and courtesies all centered on our best efforts to treat others kindly and fairly!

Since the earliest civilizations, religious people and philosophers, as well as just ordinary people of good hearts and intentions, have tried to define an ideal universal path of fair, livable choices for human interaction.

In countries and cultures around the world, the simple premise of seeking to *treat others as you would have them treat you* has been determined to be a prime guideline for personal actions.

Platinum-Silver-Gold

This attempt at finding the ethical way of interacting with others has been called by many names, such as the *Platinum Rule*, the *Silver Rule* and perhaps the most famous and well-known, *The Golden Rule*. The Golden Rule's principle of conduct is found with great similarity of expression in the cultures of ancient Egypt, Greece, Persia, China, India and Judea, to name a few. It lives today in one form or another and is called by various names in the religions and philosophies throughout the world.

Circulating Kindness!

In our Etiquette of Kindness, practice of the principle of The Golden Rule applies to not only our own in-group, our own family, friends or community, but also to how we treat everyone!

Our efforts to treat others decently and justly are alive and energetic — linking us with countless other people today as well as throughout history in the noble effort of trying to ensure that *what goes around and comes around* is kindness and fairness! This timeless and universal endeavor is *circular* and *free-flowing* in its nature. Thereby, when with our best efforts we give and receive and give and receive and give…kindness, we are a vital part of the ongoing legacy of *circulating kindness!*

By any name or title, this *rule* of trying to interact in kindness is the best, the highest basis for everything we do! It's what we are learning and practicing here in the Etiquette of Kindness!

It's *Simple! Not Always Easy* — But *So* Worthwhile!

We know by history that everyone has not always held to this ideal of living and acting!

We know that we ourselves don't always act within our own best intentions of kindness, compassion, courtesy, understanding and honesty.

However, we also know that we can always begin again, each moment, to do better and to live more fully in trying to treat others as we believe we would like to be treated in any given situation.

In our efforts to be kind in all actions, we also understand that:

- We cannot know the inner thoughts and desires of every person.

- We cannot experience the real *living* of every tradition, religion and cultural community that helps to shape people.

We know that we will make mistakes, both in our determinations and in our actions!

We may have the best of intentions, but since we can never actually *be* the other person, live their experiences or get into their head or heart, we will sometimes come up short in our desires and actions to do the right thing by others.

Always Learning in Kindness

But, here's the bottom line for our purposes in our Etiquette of Kindness:

> No matter our shortcomings and mistakes, we will do our best to act in kindness, compassion, honesty and fairness as we go along, learning in Life. When we mess up (and it *will* happen!), we will gratefully and humbly begin again, in the moment, to act more fully out of our Etiquette of Kindness.

In trying to live in actions of kindness, consideration and fairness, we will remember to use our *key tools* in determining how to treat others well:

- We will *ask* what others need and want.

- We will *listen* to their views and needs.

- We will *share* our ideas and requirements.

- We will *work* together!

- We will *apologize* when we get it wrong.

- We will *accept* the apologies of others.

- We will *renew* our seeking of ways to honor and respect others!

And, we are encouraged and ennobled in our efforts when we remember that we are in great company! We are part of billions of people who, from the beginnings of human history right up through today and into the future, have tried, are trying and will try to act from *The Etiquette of Kindness!* That's a powerful group for goodness! *Yaaay,* us!

Research and Discussion Opportunities:

For those students, parents and teachers who are interested in further exploration on this topic, look up the histories of the *Golden Rule*, the *Platinum* and *Silver Rule* and other *rules and* ideas of the ways to live that have been sought and contemplated by the ancient and modern religions, traditions and philosophies.

Think about and discuss the problems and arguments, successes and failures experienced by people through the ages as they tried to figure out the *right ways* to act toward each other.

Discuss that there have been in the past, and are today, some who argue that there is no real way to determine a *golden rule of actions.* Research their reasoning and then have a conversation around what you find and around your feelings, questions, convictions and opinions.

After you have completed reading and as you put into practice *The Etiquette of Kindness*, revisit the idea of there being *no* valid way of determining a *precious rule of conduct,* be that the Golden Rule or a rule by any name. Discuss what you observe and your opinions in light of what you have learned and are experiencing. Reconsider and discuss whether you now think that such a rule of conduct could ever be made alive and vital enough to serve a large number of people across many religions and ethnic areas.

Make It Personal:

• Talk about your family's religious or belief history and about how your immediate family and any known ancestors have chosen to try to live in kindness, honesty and fairness.

• Students, ask your parents and teachers to tell you stories of people they know personally, or relatives in your or their family, who they feel have shown great kindness to others. You'll undoubtedly find some *family and friend heroes* and *sheroes* when you discuss this together!

• Consider making an *Our Family's History of Kindness* in which you write down the tales of outstanding personal examples of kindness, fairness and honesty that people in your own family have shown! (Maybe include photos, any news clippings, mementos or illustrations you might like to create.) I believe you and your family will be surprised at how many of your relatives have shown – and currently show – real examples of living in generosity and kindness!

19.

Inspired By Our Etiquette Of Kindness!

Words for Possible Contemplation and Discussion...

Words can inspire and motivate! Words can help us to reflect on our actions and to qualify how we want to live.

Spend some time looking at the following list; add your own. Find ways to make these words and the qualities they inspire alive and vital in daily living!

Strong

Patient

Kind

Creative

Quiet

Courteous

Considerate

Perceptive

Balanced

Resourceful

Mindful

Honest

Observant

Respectful

Fun

Humorous

Expressive

Fair

Vibrant

Wise

Seeking

Prayerful

Peaceful

Willing

Flexible

Loving

Generous

Innovative

Truthful

Sensitive

Valiant

Appreciative

Enduring

Soulful

Spiritual

Joyful

Open

Appropriate

Outgoing

Contemplative

Inspiring

Reliable

Discerning

Intelligent

Helpful

Caring

Courageous

Faithful

Solid

Grateful

Innovative

Responsible

Honorable

Steadfast

Contemplation and Discussion Opportunities:

Add to this list! Pick a few to research their meanings; think about them on your own or discuss with family and friends.

Consider people you know who seem to exhibit a special proportion of some of these traits or attributes.

Which of these words do you believe might especially describe yourself?

Which of these would you like to expand as qualities you exemplify?

20.

Final Thoughts

(Because I think you're terrific!)

As I said at the beginning of our Etiquette of Kindness journey, "Who would have guessed that there could be such passion hidden in etiquette!" But, indeed that is what I've found to be the case. In my estimation, there's nothing more exciting in Life than to experience people joining together to make good things happen for themselves, for others and for their surroundings! And, that's precisely what we do in our Etiquette of Kindness.

We've seen and discussed here that not everyone necessarily looks at what we may consider to be "kindness" or "good etiquette" just as we do. Trying to put into practice The Golden Rule or any general rule of kindness, consideration, manners, conduct and courtesy is not always simple. But! We always try to do our best – and then, we try again…and again…

In our efforts to be kind and to act in ways that are courteous and inoffensive to others, we get a LOT right, some things right enough, and a few things we resolve to work on or revisit with new knowledge – and humility!

We've experienced that kindness is *circular*, that to the best of our ability, it's an *I-Thou* recognition of each human being in respect, courtesy and consideration. We realize that any good deed flows out in intertwining circles, much like the ripples on the lake, influencing and enhancing as it flows!

And, we've learned that we can cut each other slack for our "Oops!" and our mistakes and poor choices — and that we sure appreciate it when others show us similar allowances! As caring people, we know that mistakes can be wonderful opportunities to seek better choices, to gain skills and to learn patience with ourselves and with others.

We've learned, too, when to stand firm and that, for instance, *bullying* — by us, by anyone — is *never okay!* We never support the bad acts; we always speak up! We are courageous; together we are a Courageous Community of Kindness, making a difference, making bullying less and less of a problem — less and less an actuality!

We've seen and experienced how our *Attitude of Gratitude* and a ready smile can work wonders for us — and for others. We've realized that gratitude for even the smallest of things can transform this very moment, this very day! And, we treasure the great gifts that are our families, our friends, our teachers — all who love, guide and help us. With open, appreciative hearts and minds we are generous in our thoughts of others; we *act* out of our gratitude and joy!

Along with our super-serious subjects, we've had some laughs and gained skills in everyday endeavors of making life smoother, more fun and more enjoyable for ourselves and for others.

We've *certainly* learned which fork to choose for what!

We've learned how to set a nice table, how to conduct ourselves as a guest or as a host and how to create pleasant introductions and memorable, satisfying conversations. We've gained skills in ways to present ourselves with courtesy, kindness and self-confidence, expressing ourselves well when we speak and when we write.

E-devices in our hands will not be threats to others! We know when and how to courteously (and safely!) use our cell phones, tablets and all of our electronic ways through which we keep in touch with our friends and with our world!

We are skilled — and looking forward to gaining more skills and refinements as we go along, widening our world, meeting new acquaintances and making new friends!

So, my young friends, I think you're terrific! You're strong of heart and of mind, and you've got what it takes to *live* our Etiquette of Kindness. Do your best in everything! Be grateful! Enjoy! Gain skills, be kindly, show compassion — have fabulous lives and be a light to your world! Leave a *legacy of love* in your footsteps!

I wish *us all* the very best in our daily adventures of choosing a path of kindness; for one good thing flows into another and another... and who knows where our *actions* of good intentions may lead us?

With affection and respect,

Suzanne-Marie English

My Own Thanks

I'm a firm believer in the concept and the practical actualities of "It takes a village…" – especially when it comes to making kinder, more courteous choices and more caring and respectful relationships. Since my book, *The Etiquette of Kindness – It's Not Just About the Right Fork!* stems from our interactions as human beings, I have specific thanks to offer. Whether by intent, by simply being an inspiration in my life or by a combination of both factors, everyone mentioned here helped me to make this book a reality. Because of you, The Etiquette of Kindness *movement* has begun!

My gratitude begins with the engaged, warm and welcoming teachers and students with whom I've been privileged to share our Etiquette Classes over the past fourteen years.

To the wonderful students who welcomed me with grace and courtesy – thank you! Each day that we interacted, laughed and "got" our message of etiquette, was a delight for me! Thank you for making it so easy to share my passion for door-opening Life skills with you all. You are terrific and I hold the memory of each of you in my heart and in my mind. I always wish you the very best and think of you "out there" making good, kindly, productive things happen for yourselves – and for others!

I am in awe of the many great teachers over the years who have so generously shared their precious class time and their students with me as we broadened our etiquette skills together. I thank each of you for these gifts and for your trust and confidence. Observing the depth, heart, skill, dignity, verve and wisdom you bring to education – to students, parents and to other teachers – has been an honor and an inspiration!

Special gratitude is due to my friend, Janet Langley, who is a respected master teacher. Years ago, Janet, you first gave me the opportunity to share my concept of Etiquette Classes for young people. With warmth you welcomed me into your eighth grade class; what an opportunity that was! Over the passing years, from that first class and with subsequent classes of sixth, seventh and eighth graders, you've been unfailingly enthusiastic and encouraging. I so value your expertise, your friendship and our enjoyable times shared in your classrooms. Thank you for everything, Janet!

I am also grateful to you, Amy Elder, Matt Taylor, Paula Thompson and Lisa Morgan. It's been delightful to work with each of you incredibly dedicated, inspired and hard-working teachers! Thank you for giving me the opportunities to share my Etiquette Classes with your students. I've learned much from observing you as teachers, and I thank you for your friendship and your enthusiastic support!

Sometimes, geographical distance prevented me from personally sharing the Etiquette Class series with students and teachers farther away. But, distance doesn't stop a devoted teacher! To each of you enthusiastic teachers who called or wrote, wanting to *talk etiquette,* thank you. I loved our conversations, your questions and observations. With each contact I further realized how this book could help spread the word and work of *The Etiquette of Kindness.* Thank you for reaching out!

My thanks to skilled, talented teachers who have taught me so much simply by my association with them, wouldn't be complete without expressing gratitude to one more: superlative teacher and dear friend, Patti Connolly. Patti, your teaching of our youngest son was not only a huge gift to him, but to our entire family. It was in you that I first recognized what a thoroughly gifted teacher could be, full of heart, soul, *cellular* dedication, fun, dignity, deep intuitive wisdom and brilliance. Thank you, Patti, for being a wonderful friend to me and a beloved and loving pivotal influence in our family!

For over a year, I knew pretty much what I wanted as illustrations for *The Etiquette of Kindness* – and, there was never a question of whether or not there would be illustrations! From covers through chapters, I saw in my mind's eye the *look,* the layout and the silhouetted figures of Kindness Kids interacting. It lived well in my head, but finding the artist...? Thank you, my friend, Risha Rose, for connecting me with Alexander Orion Sparks. As they say, "the rest is history!"

What a fun, satisfying, enjoyable collaboration it's been with you, Al. Working with you – from illustration concepts through decisions to bringing the finished Kindness Kids onto the cover and pages – has been a delightful experience! And, every aspect has been on time and drama-free! I couldn't have asked for a more sensitive, skilled, enthusiastic artist. You got the sense of fun and spirit that I tried to convey – you got it every time – and you brought fresh "takes", inventive "spins" and great ideas. What I had *seen,* you took and made so much better – thank you. I'm proud of our Kindness Kids crew you brought to form!

Silke Rose, former language teacher, longtime friend and my incredibly patient, expert editor, I thank you for your clear, steadfast help. How many times did you patiently say: "Well, I know what you are saying, but, for me, the words in this sentence just aren't doing it!" All through our many editing hours, you never imposed your thoughts on me, but respected and worked with my own style while we achieved greater clarity – and removed, among a few other punctuation tidbits, all extraneous ellipses. (Sigh!) That old phrase, "Thanks, I needed that!" certainly applied to all your editing efforts with me. Thank you, Silke!

A huge "Thank you!" to my friends – Peggy C. Papathakis, PhD, RD; Brad Barnhill, MD; Raissa M. Hill, DO; Anne Bucon, LCSW; and Kay Osborn,

RN, NPT (retired) — all health professionals, parents and, in some cases, grandparents! I know that each of you is dedicated to enhancing the health, happiness and welfare of children — not only those of your own family, but also a whole collective "legion" of children with whom you've been involved professionally and in your many selfless endeavors for communities. Having the benefit of your eyes and expert knowledge has been a critical help in my determining which general health and wellness suggestions I can wisely make to our young people. Thank you for all you do in Life — and for graciously stepping forward in my request for critique of sections of my book dealing with healthful choices and interactions. I so appreciate your can-do spirit, your kindness and generosity with your time and expertise. Thank you, again!

To Dave Garner of *Shebang Creative!* for your years of fun, loving and kindly family friendship and now for having generously agreed to take on my website creation, I thank you! Your never-failing patience, your sense of humor, your fabulous artistic eye and your professional expertise I value highly. Thank you for taking my message seriously and for helping to get it launched online.

To my husband, Richard, and son, John: Thank you for all of your enthusiastic, unwavering support of my work, for your critiques, the humor and good spirit you've brought when I needed it and the terrific ideas you've shared with me. John, your help with all things computer, website and online technical have been invaluable! Thank you both for helping me to make *The Etiquette of Kindness* a reality; this book never would have made it to the publisher without you!

For my mother, Elizabeth: Somewhere a couple of months into my actually writing this book, you happened to passionately relate to me "The one thing that I've learned over my long life is to just try to *be kind!*" We talked of the simplicity — and the challenge — of actually doing this in daily life. And, I realized that when I boiled down all I'd been sharing with the classes of kids over the years, *kindness* was at the center of everything we'd been learning and defining together. Thus, *The Etiquette of Kindness* title and the clearer focus of my book. Thank you!

To *each* of our adult children: Whether as kindly, engaged, fun aunts and uncles building family ties, or as dedicated, loving, wisdom-seeking parents,

I honor your thorough commitment to your (our!) children; it's wonderful to see. "Thank you!" from me – and from the world that receives your kids!

And, to each of our grandchildren: you are great fun and inspiring in your beauty of being and in your loving generosity. You all have bright futures and I wish you the very best now and forever! Keep gaining skills, keep making excellent choices, keep doing your very best in all things – and keep sharing your lives with those who love you. I'm proud of you!

To my friends, old and new: I've learned so much from each of you in your interactions with others. Whether I expressed it at the time or reflected on it later over months or years and whether directed toward me or another, I noted your expressions of compassion and your many kindnesses. I appreciate you. Thank you!

The Author
The Illustrator

For fourteen years, Suzanne-Marie English has brought Etiquette Classes to sixth, seventh and eighth graders. Working with the children and their teachers, helping to identify and refine etiquette skills and manners and sharing with young people ways to interact kindly and courteously has been a delight and passion for her. Long a writer of poetry and short stories, Suzanne-Marie took seriously the requests of numerous parents and teachers to put the Etiquette Classes into book form. Thus, *The Etiquette of Kindness – It's Not Just About the Right Fork!* came to be written.

Suzanne-Marie is a mother of four and, together with her husband, Richard English, is a grandparent of nine. She and her family live in the foothills of the Northern California Sierras. She may be contacted through the *Etiquette of Kindness* website: www.etiquetteofkindness.com

Alexander Orion Sparks is currently completing his degree as a concept artist at San Jose State University. His passion for observation suffuses his artwork and guides his studies in science, philosophy and world affairs. He can often be found painting at a local coffee shop, if he is not programming, acting, or playing ukulele. Alexander's artworks can be seen at his web address: alexandersparks.blogspot.com

CPSIA information can be obtained at www.ICGtesting.com
Printed in the USA
LVOW09s2235050516

486936LV00007B/23/P

9 781479 181407